THE BOOK

LECTOR HOUSE PUBLIC DOMAIN WORKS

THE BOOK

CYRIL DAVENPORT

9 789354 208973

ISBN: 978-93-5420-897-3

Published: 1907

LECTOR HOUSE LLP
E-MAIL: lectorpublishing@gmail.com

**Golden Binding of "The Gospels of Charlemagne," with Jewels
and Enamels, 11th or 12th Century.**

[Frontispiece.

[See page 43.

THE BOOK
ITS HISTORY AND DEVELOPMENT

BY

CYRIL DAVENPORT, V.D. F.S.A.

ILLUSTRATED

1907

CONTENTS

LIST OF PLATES

THE BOOK

CHAPTER I.

EARLY RECORDS.

Rock inscriptions—Marks on wood—Quipus—Wampum—Modern ideographs—Indian palm leaf books—Ideographs and alphabets—Diptychs.

The idea of making records by means of marks cut on stone or wood did not originate in any one place, for signs of it are found more or less all over the world wherever primitive man has existed. It was not until a comparatively late period that the various kinds of record keeping were unified after a fashion and true writing evolved itself out of the chaos.

There are some forms of record keeping that have been largely used by the human race which, as far as we can at present tell, have not influenced our present form of book except negatively; but indirectly they may still have done so in some manner that we cannot distinguish.

Mankind is naturally imitative, and among his early efforts in this direction are the scratchings on bones and antlers. They comprise outlines of deer, mammoths, reindeer, seals, bears, horses and other animals. Several instances of these early drawings have been found in the caves of the Dordogne in France. These, however, are not records, they are only pictures of what the artist saw, and a large proportion of rock and stone markings come into the same category. But there is no doubt that many of the latter are intended to commemorate certain events; they show groupings of marks, animals and men in positions and attitudes which are clearly intended to mean something, and now and then it has been possible to make a good guess at their interpretation.

The earliest marks made by man that still exist are to be found among the rock markings or carvings, as these are often in protected places where the weather has not worn them away. Prehistoric caves and tombs are prolific in such treasures, and the marks, ideographs or hieroglyphics are always of the greatest interest. There seems to be some analogy between the great megalithic temples like that on Salisbury Plain and many of the rock inscriptions, but little is at present known on this point.

Cup and ring markings on rocks or stones are among the most remarkable of rock inscriptions because they are not isolated as to their design. From Ireland to India these marks are found possessing the same radical forms, and it is impossible to avoid the conclusion that they have been made by tribes of men who had some thought or idea in common. What this idea was is still a disputed point among archæologists.

Cup and ring markings are held by some authorities to be astronomical, sun signs, but these speculations, especially in Scandinavian examples, soon land us in pure symbolism, ring crosses, swastikas, triskeles and the rest.

Apart from these, marks are found in the British Isles and in India particularly through which a dominant idea is clearly present. It seems likely that some common religious symbolism is really the key to the mystery, and this belief, disavowed by Sir J. Simpson, is strongly held by Col. J. H. Rivett-Carnac, as well as by many others. By these archæologists the cup and ring markings are considered to be the ideographic expressions of one of the primitive religions of the world which was very widely spread, and the remains of which exist in India at the present day.

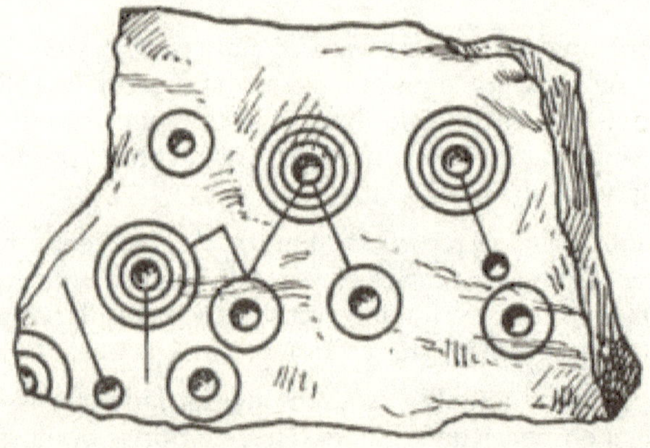

Fig. 1.—Stone cist with ring marks. Found at Coilsford in Ayrshire.

But even admitting the possibility of this interpretation, there are still many points left unexplained. For instance, in the drawing, it will be seen that the cups with their rings are cunningly attached to each other, and the whole design appears as if it "means something." No doubt some day further light will be thrown upon this curious form of record.

The Assyrian and Babylonian sculptures both in the round and in bas-reliefs are commonly covered with cuneiform inscriptions, and these are also plentifully found inscribed on stone stelæ and bronze figurines. The famous Rosetta stone is a familiar example of a tri-lingual inscription that will probably last as long as the world lasts. It is now in the British Museum, and bears an inscription in Hieroglyphic, Demotic and Greek. The Greek being understood, it gave at once the key to the interpretation of the Hieroglyphic. The date of the cutting of this stone is about the beginning of the second century before the birth of Christ. An earlier stone of a similar kind is known as the tablet of Sen; it contains a decree of the priests at Canopus in honour of Ptolemy Evergetes I. It was made in B.C. 238, but has not yet got to England.

The ten commandments were engraved on stone, and instances of inscriptions on small stones are very numerous. From Egypt to North America amulets bearing mystical sentences have been commonly made. Familiar to most of us are the turquoises engraved with Arabic words run in with gold, and the curious "Garuda" and other stones, with magical inscriptions and credited with magical powers, have been common in the East from time immemorial.

Fig. 2.—Garuda amulet.

In India inscriptions, holy names, invocations and quotations are cut on small flat pieces of jasper, agate, onyx, carnelian, amethyst, hematite, jade, and materials of less value like coral or glass, some of the old and some new. Musulman amulets of similar kinds are also sometimes found on gold, silver, iron, and even on small bricks of baked clay.

Many of these amulets have pierced ears for suspension, and they were worn as jewellery on the neck or ears or sewn on girdles. They were also fixed on weapons of war and horse furniture. Some of the stones are engraved in reverse so as to make impressions. These are seal stones, but the greater number are engraved simply so as to read straightforwardly. They are in Arabic, Persian, and rarely Turkish.

Greek and Roman cameos and intaglios are often found bearing short inscriptions as well as the names of their engravers. Even the diamond has not escaped, but inscriptions on this stone are very rare because of the difficulty of engraving it. Numbers of inscriptions, names and mottoes can be found on ring stones of all times as well as on real stones.

Curious Chinese books are made of leaves of jade, and in these inscriptions are cut in the decorative Chinese character, run in with gold.

It should be noted that the forms of letters have always been much influenced by the manner in which they could be most easily made. It is easier to cut a square form of letter on stone than a cursive form, so we find that the majority of rock or stone inscriptions favour the square form rather than the rounded form of letter. We derive our angular forms of letters from the distant past, but the rounded forms are adapted from the later times of papyrus or vellum, when reed or pen writing was understood.

Writings on metal have been made from time to time, but never very largely. In India inscribed plaques of bronze, kept together by metal rings, have been often used. Tablets of lead are recorded as having been used by ancient peoples, and Oriental as well as European talismanic formulæ have been engraved on small plates of silver, bronze, brass or lead, the letters being now and then damascened with gold and silver. In ancient Rome name-brands were cut in bronze, and impressions could have been printed from them. They were beautifully cut.

The Nicene creed was cut in silver by order of Pope Leo III., and in the East strips of metal have constantly been substituted for the long thin pieces of palm leaf which formed the normal books. The metal leaves are found of gold, silver, or gilded copper particularly. The plates are quite thin, and the characters upon them are generally engraved, but sometimes they are chased with tracer and hammer. Such records are not only very permanent but they are also very decorative. The modern engraving of inscriptions on metal has mainly found refuge in monumental brasses, and in this case the letterings are usually run in with some pigment.

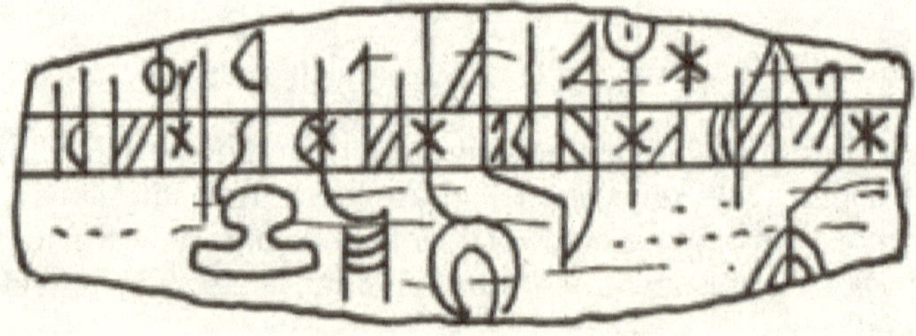

Fig. 3.—Runic calendar on bone.

Another primitive form of record is found in the case of notches cut in wood. A savage warrior of a literary turn of mind would naturally wish to keep some record of the number of his enemies that he had killed and perhaps eaten, and an obvious way of doing this would be to cut or scratch marks on his war club. Such records would, no doubt, become customary among war-like tribes. The handles of war axes or spears would offer excellent ground for such marks, and presently, especially in peace times, similar marks may well have kept tallies of the numbers of game killed.

From such personal notes the transition to others of wider interest is not difficult, and so we find the notches used, on bits of wood or sticks, for almanacks and calendars.

Ogham and Runic inscriptions follow the ancient idea of notches cut along an angular edge, and these notches and rods are the very distant ancestors of our modern types of metal; the German word "Buchstab," meaning type, is etymologically "a wooden rod."

In Denmark and Sweden in ancient times almanacks were cut on flat pieces of metal, bone, horn, box, fir or oak. The majority of them are of wood, but the other materials were sometimes used. They are variously known as Rune staves or stocks, Prime staves, Messe dag staves or Brim stocks, and they are generally hinged along one side by cords run through holes, several slabs being thus fastened together. Wooden calendars are also often found among the records kept by primitive peoples; they have been found in Sumatra and in many other places.

Similar almanacks were used by our Saxon ancestors, who no doubt borrowed the idea from the Scandinavians. One side was kept for the summer and the other for the winter, and notches for the days were made across the edges.

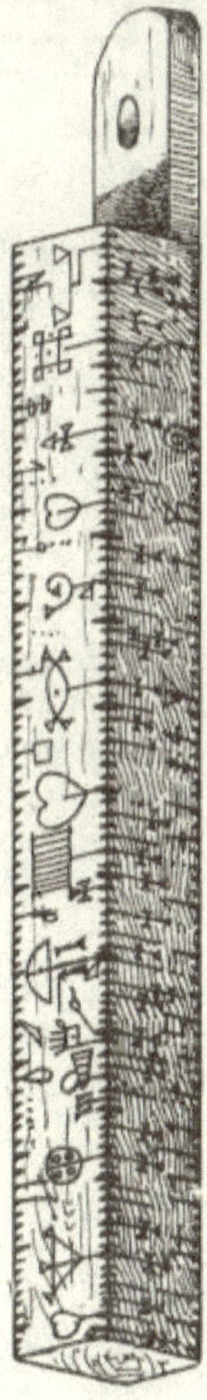

Fig. 4. — Staffordshire clog almanack.

During the reign of Queen Elizabeth a modification of the Scandinavian Rune staves was largely used in England, chiefly in Staffordshire, but not exclusively. These are known as "clog almanacks," and Dr. Plott says that "Clogg may mean Logg, or that they are like the cloggs with which we restrain our doggs."

English clog almanacks are squared pieces of wood, measuring from about two feet to nine or ten inches in length, and the larger ones are sometimes as much as three inches square. They are notched along the angles, small notches without ornamentation indicating week days, big notches stand for Sundays, and Saints days have all kinds of ornamental flourishes, which now and then show familiar forms such as Saint Catherine's wheel and Saint Lawrence's gridiron.

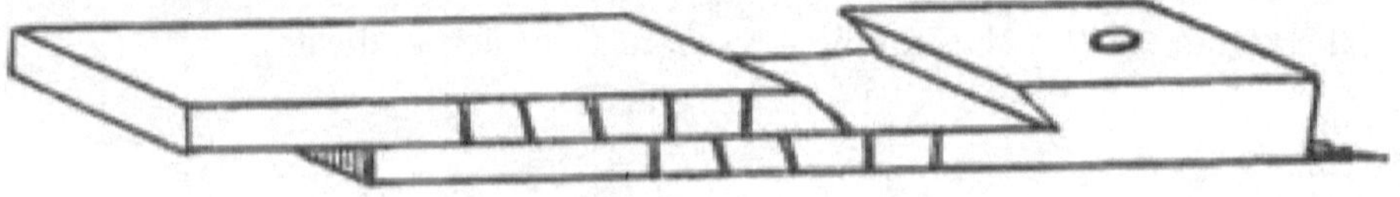

Fig. 5.—Modern hop-tally of wood.

Some of the clogs show a hole at the lower end, evidently so that they could stand upright upon a peg, others, and these are the most usual, have a flat pierced handle so that they can be suspended by a loop. They were commonly kept in churches. Details of several well known examples of clog almanacks will be found figured in *The Reliquary* for January, 1865, in illustration of an excellent article on the subject by Mr. John Harland. Exchequer and other wooden tallies were common in England in the 14th century, and in modern days a certain survival of them exists in the form of hop-tallies. These are two strips of wood which fit closely together with a tongue, and when in contact notches are made across the two edges in apposition, so that when the two pieces are apart, neither party can falsify the notches without it being at once apparent when the slips are finally brought together. The principle is exactly the same as that utilised in the old legal "indentures," by virtue of which a piece of vellum was cut in two by an indentured, or toothed line, and if these did not exactly fit whenever they were brought together it became evident that they had been tampered with. In parts of France tallies like these are still used by bakers.

Wooden tallies are also found among the inhabitants of Torres Straits, where they use them made of short sticks tied together at their tops.

Curious inscriptions, as yet undecipherable, have been found at Easter Island; they are cut in thick slabs of wood and are ideographic.

Bones have been from very early times the recipients of men's marks; the earliest of these, however, were only copies of things seen. But inscriptions and symbols were presently scratched on them, and the blade bones of buffaloes in North America as well as the shoulder blades of sheep used by the Arabs are equally convenient for writing upon. In Sumatra inscriptions are commonly cut in flat pieces of bone. Instances of inscriptions in ivory are very numerous, and the finest examples of these occur in the case of the Roman consular diptychs which are described a little further on.

Information as to direction is still often given by means of marks or "blazes" on trees, a survival of a primitive method, and American lumbermen or "loggers" cut hieroglyphic marks of ownership on their logs when they send them down stream.

In times of trouble it often happens that primitive methods of communication are resorted to, like that received by a Cavalier from his lady love who heard that the Roundheads were after him—she sent him a feather, and he flew away and escaped.

Fig. 6.

Such symbolical messages are common enough among savage tribes, but without some key it is almost impossible to interpret them. They are so various in their composition that no useful analysis of them can be made. On one such message from West Africa, strung on a string of flat fibre knotted at each end, are a bit of shell, a bit of fur, a bean, a cylindrical stick, a piece of leather, a mass of frog's eggs or something like it, a flat piece of bark, a feather, a tooth and a shell. In another are two pieces of flat glass kept together with red thread, and two teeth on each side of it, all strung on fibre, and so on.

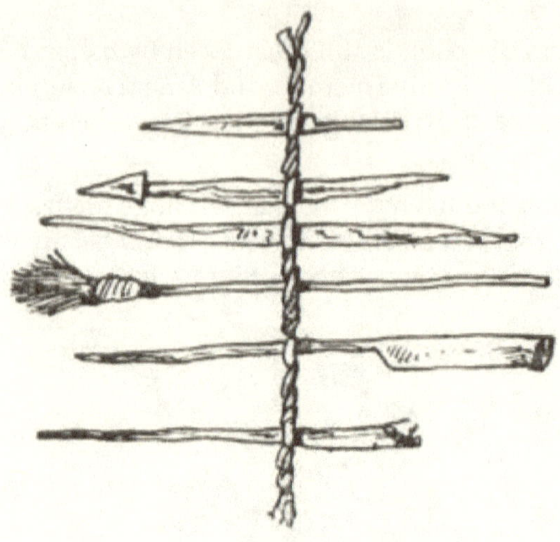

Fig. 7.

The Battas of Sumatra use different and probably more elaborate messages, as they consist of carefully cut strips of wood, resembling the old spillikins with which our childhood's days were made happy. These strips of thin wood, about three inches in length, are cut into various shapes which have no obvious collective meaning. In one of them is a capital model of a little broom, accompanied apparently by a series of little clubs and spikes. Such a message might have been sent by an absent brave to his squaw at home, and may have meant that if she didn't sweep up the wigwam before his arrival she would experience the effect of one or other of the clubs.

The Incas of Peru had a regular system of keeping records by means of coloured pieces of string knotted in a peculiar way.

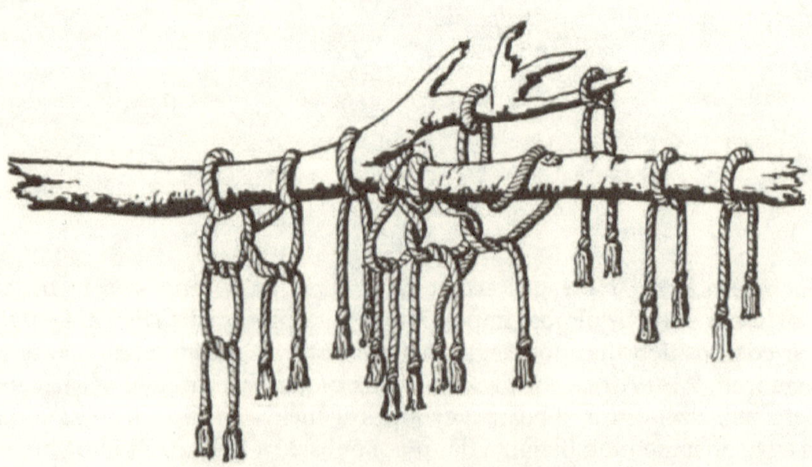

Fig. 8.—Peruvian Quipu.

These knotted records, or Quipus, had special keepers who held office in the provinces, and the results of their energy were forwarded annually to the capital city for examination and preservation. The provincial keepers were called "Quipu Camayas," and the records they kept were mainly statistics concerning the people of their districts. The knots were arranged either on a strong piece of cord or upon a stick, and formed a sort of fringe; the word "Quipu" means a knot. According to the position of the knot a certain number was probably indicated, and the class of person referred to is shown by the colour of the bit of string which represents it.

But it is also likely that more elaborate interpretations could be made by skilled interpreters of Quipus. Little is really known as to that, but it is suggested by competent observers that, for instance, red meant war, yellow meant gold, white meant peace, and silver. But this is probably guess work. The same idea has been utilised in the case of a rare Chinese book, the leaves of which were of differently coloured silks. Each colour was supposed to convey a certain emotion to the student, and when he had exhausted the emotion caused by one colour, he turned over the leaf so as to experience the effect of another.

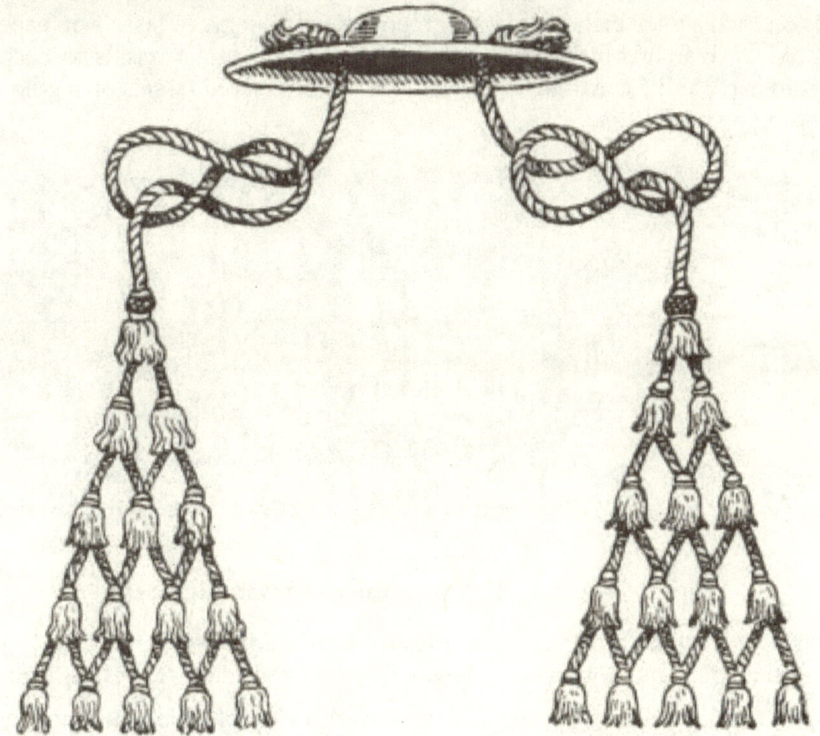

Fig. 9.—Cardinal's hat.

The use of knots as reminders is not quite obsolete, as it is common enough even now to make a knot in one's handkerchief, if anything easy is to be remembered. It is curious if this custom is really a survival of the Peruvian Quipu!

A form of knotted record is used among several of the tribes in the Pacific Islands, and the Jewish "Taleth," or scarf, has fringes which imply certain facts.

The ordinary rosary with its ten beads for Ave Maria's and single ones for Pater Nosters has also something in common with knots, and possibly the abacus of the Greeks and the Chinese may have a similar origin. But probably these last are only used as aids in mathematical calculations.

Something analogous to the Peruvian knots is to be found in the tasselled and knotted fringes which adorn the ceremonial hats of dignitaries in the Romish church.

The hats themselves are always of the same shape, round shallow crowns with broad brims. The fringes, however, differ in size and colour according to the rank of the wearer. The master cord is drawn through the brim of the hat at its inner edge, at a point over each ear, and kept in place by a large ornamental knot on the outside.

The tassels start from one, and from this two others depend, and from these three, and so on, one more in each row. An abbot wears a black hat with six green tassels on each side; a bishop wears a green hat with six green tassels on each side on a gold cord; an archbishop has a violet hat with ten violet tassels on each side on a gold cord, and a cardinal has a red hat with fifteen red tassels on a gold cord, depending on each side.

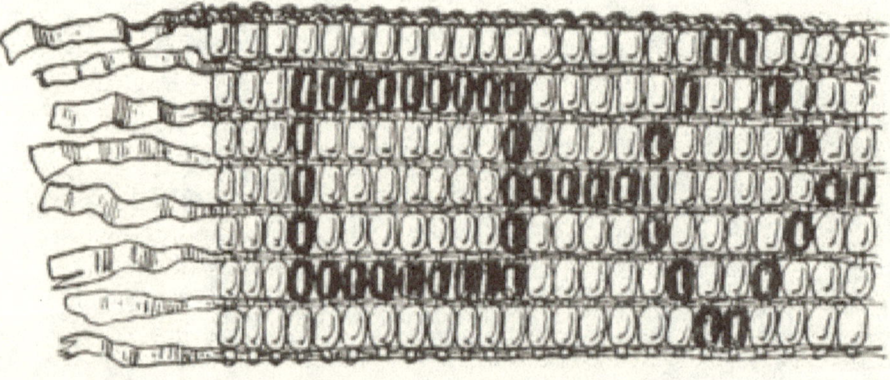

Fig. 10.—Portion of North American wampum belt.

The wampum belts of North America were primarily used as money, but they were also made sometimes in such a way that they formed historical records.

The true "Six Nation" wampum belts were made of little white and purple cylinders of shell very laboriously cut, and the purple ones very difficult to get. "Wampum" means white, and there is generally a preponderance of this colour. The short beads are strung upon long threads or strips of leather, and the design shows sometimes in purple on a white ground and sometimes in white on a purple ground.

The designs are sometimes easy to decipher, like the belt which typifies the

Iroquois League, showing the one heart of the ruling nation in the centre, and the allied nations, each shown by a square, united together in one bond.

A very fine and interesting wampum belt was given as a record of friendship to William Penn at the Great Treaty in 1682, by the Sachems of the Lenni Lenape. It is now preserved by the Historical Society at Philadelphia. It is made of eighteen rows of white and purple cylindrical shell beads, the ground white and the designs in purple. The beads are laced upon nineteen parallel "horizontal" strips of leather by means of thinner strips running vertically across them and brought twice through each bead, one running being above the horizontal strip and the other below it. It is a curious way of stringing beads, and was practised in England some sixty or seventy years ago in the making of small bead ribbons. In the centre of the belt is a conventional figure of Penn shaking hands with the chief Sachem.

Many of the wampum belts seem to have only geometrical designs upon them, but doubtless, without exception, these fine white and purple shell belts, cut with infinite patience and skill, and put together with the greatest care, always have some meaning. The Iroquois could, until recently, interpret them at once, but now they are less able to understand the work of their ancestors.

There are plenty of imitation wampum belts, usually made of small shells or ordinary beads. The genuine belts are flat and strong, and the little shell cylinders nearly all of the same size. The imitations are much more irregularly and carelessly made, and they are often without any colour but white.

A common form of book in Oriental countries consists of long narrow strips of palm leaf, kept together by two strings run through holes near each end. The writing upon the leaves is carried right along the length of each leaf in successive lines, and is scratched in, and usually strengthened by means of lamp black rubbed over it so as to stick in the scratches.

Fig. 11.—Oriental palm-leaf book.

This form of book rests by itself. Apparently it has never altered materially, neither has it in any way affected the production of the book as we know it. The palm leaves are brittle, they are troublesome to turn over, and are likely to split and break where the cord touches them. But the leaves are frequently made of stronger materials than palm leaf, some of them being of gold, silver, or gilded copper, and in these cases the lettering is engraved or punched. Others are written on plates of ivory, the letters being gilded, others again on plates of lacquer with letters inlaid with mother-of-pearl; indeed, the variety is large.

The leaves are always enclosed between two covers of stronger make but of the same shape, and these covers are often very elaborately ornamented. Some of them have exquisite carved work and inlaid work and others are painted. In the case of Indian examples they are often messed over with red stains. When this is found the manuscript has belonged to some shrine, and worshippers have daubed it with rice and red paint as a sort of peace offering. The strings with which the leaves are bound together are also sometimes handsomely ornamented.

Ancient rock inscriptions, tallies, quipus and wampums are all more or less ideographic, and among trade signs there are still many ideographs in common use, some of them of considerable antiquity. There are the three golden balls of the pawnbroker, which mean that money can be borrowed there. They are derived from the coat of arms of the Medici of Lombardy. The Lombards were mediæval bankers and money lenders, and for their badge they took three of the golden balls, or pills, out of the Medici coat.

These balls varied in number and colour, they were sometimes red, and sometimes blue, and three blue balls upon a white ground was one of the mediæval signs used by money lenders, but the three golden balls have proved more lasting.

Another old ideograph is the white barber's pole, with its red spiral, the image of the red bandage used to tie up an arm which had just been bled. It was originally the mark of a barber surgeon, but the barber still uses it although he no longer bleeds his clients. An old sign for a barber is also a shaving dish. This is oftener seen on the continent than it is here.

The embowed arm holding a hammer is an old sign of a gold beater, and is generally itself gilded. It is clearly an ideograph, as is also the fishing rod with a golden fish, which is a usual sign over a fishing tackle maker's shop. A modern instance of the same kind is a gilded ham which is not uncommonly seen over provision shops, quite a modern sign. The rapidly disappearing Highlander taking snuff is another modern ideograph. There are plenty more of such signs, most of which tell their story directly and simply, while others, the older ones particularly, may at first seem arbitrary, but often a little examination will reveal a simple origin.

The curious hieroglyphics still used by gypsies are no doubt derived from Egyptian hieroglyphics, and although most of them have changed considerably, a certain resemblance in some of the forms can still be traced.

Ideograms are still used in North America in out of the way places. A common mark for a cheese is a circle, and this sign was found opposite a farmer's name, but he had never had one. He did, however, owe for a grindstone, and the draughtsman clerk had forgotten to put in the centre dot which would have marked the difference between the stone and the edible.

In common use more or less all over the civilised world is the pointing hand, meaning either "Look there" or "This way."

Some signs are also ideographic in character; among these are certain of the deaf and dumb signs, and also some of the arm signals used in the navy. In the army some of the bugle calls imitate as far as possible the sounds to which they refer. For instance, the "prepare for cavalry" has some resemblance to horses galloping.

Ideographs used in written languages soon change in character. No longer do they mean simply what they portray, but the sound of its name, and then by degrees they represented the first syllable, and eventually only the first letter of its name. These changes of meaning are accompanied by changes of form, and it is very curious to trace how an apparently arbitrary letter form is really only the survival of the main lines of an ancient ideogram. There are several most interesting instances of these changes given by Dr. Isaac Taylor in his classic "History of the Alphabet," as well as by other writers on the subject, particularly Sir E. Maunde Thompson and Mr. Falconer Madan.

Egyptian inscriptions show both ideographs, hieroglyphics and alphabetic signs, as there is usually a word spelt out in syllables or letters, and at the end of it the complete word shown as a little picture. The hieroglyphics altered into a style of writing which was not so pictorial about the nineteenth century B.C., and although alphabetical symbols were actually used as early as 4,000 B.C., yet it was very many years later than this that they became of general use. The earliest piece of hieroglyphic known is cut upon stone on a tablet now preserved in the Ashmolean Museum at Oxford. It is supposed to have been made about 4,000 B.C., and on it the name of King Send is written alphabetically.

Our present alphabetic writing is by no means final, as it is even now undergoing a remarkable change, in which neither ideograph, hieroglyphic, nor alphabet plays any part. Shorthand will in time supersede our comparatively cumbrous process, and it is purely phonetic.

Chinese writing is still in the syllabic state, but the Japanese, which is formed from it, has advanced many steps towards the alphabetical stage.

The earliest handwriting known is that on the Papyrus Prisse, now in Paris. It is in Egyptian hieratic writing, and is supposed to date perhaps from about 4,000 B.C. The hieratic is a cursive form of hieroglyphic, and was used particularly by priests.

We derive our present letters "longo intervallo" from Egyptian hieroglyphics, and the history of their evolution is full of interest.

It may be well here to review rapidly how it is that we have acquired an alphabet for printing purposes which is clear, though not beautiful. Our present type shows two alphabets; one, the capital letters, are of Roman origin, the other, the small letters, are a modification of what are called Carolingian minuscules, and both alphabets have reached us through the Latin, Greek, Phœnician and Semitic.

Up to the seventh or eighth centuries in Europe the various styles of writing were in a mixed condition, but about that time the different forms of letters began to arrange themselves, and to follow distinctive lines of development in different countries.

Charlemagne interested himself in the matter, and saw that the time had arrived when something could be done towards clearing away the many difficulties which cropped up by reason of the different forms of letters which then existed. He caused careful studies to be made of existing styles so that some sort of common ground could be found. At Tours the Emperor set up a sort of Royal Commission to enquire into the matter, and at the head of it he placed a learned Englishman, Alcuin of York, who was known as a great student and was himself a calligraphist. Alcuin was trained in the beautiful Hiberno-Saxon hand, of which so many magnificent examples still remain—the Book of Kells, the Gospels of Lindisfarne, and several more.

At Tours the Carolingian minuscules, which are the direct ancestors of our small, or lower-case letters, were developed.

Our capital letters have developed themselves on different lines. They are like the ancient Roman types, which in the twelfth century had modified themselves somewhat and become very clear, and these forms commended themselves to the scribes of the Renaissance period, and underwent still more improvement in details. The early type cutters who formed their letters directly after the shapes of letters written by hand, soon saw that these capitals were not only easy to cut but were in every way the best they could find to copy.

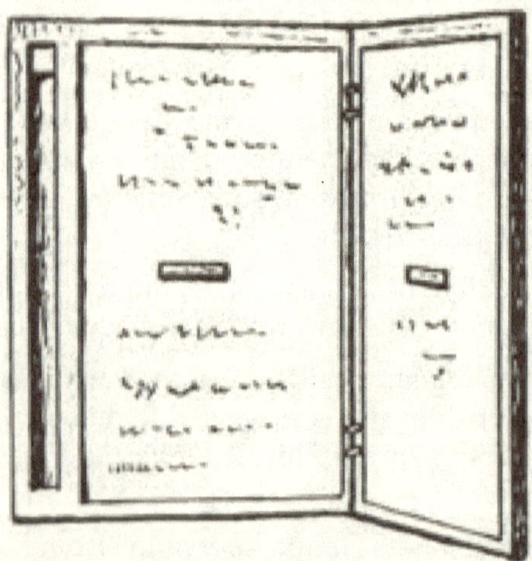

Fig. 12.—Roman diptych.

During some excavations at Pompeii in 1875 a large collection of small wax writing tablets or Pugillaria was found. These tablets resemble small slates; they are of wood, and one side is slightly hollowed out so as to receive a filling of blackened wax. Generally two of the tablets were hinged together, hence their name of diptychs, but sometimes they were in threes or even more, like a tail or "Caudex," from which it is said we derive our word Codex. Diptychs are the direct prototypes of our modern books.

The writing was marked on the wax by means of a style in the same way that writing was formerly done in England on the curious sand tables. These styles are usually of iron, sometimes inlaid with brass, but they were also made of bronze, brass, wood or bone. They always have one end pointed to write with and the other flat to erase with. A space was often left in the thickness of the wooden edge of a diptych to keep the style in. The erasing in the case of the diptych was effected by rubbing the flat end of the style over it, and in the case of the sand writing-tablet by a plasterer's level or a good shake. Sand tablets have been used up to quite recent times in elementary schools. But the sand writing was always temporary, whereas the wax writing is very lasting, one of those found at Pompeii bearing the date A.D. 55. It records a payment to Umbricia Januaria, and is the earliest Latin manuscript known.

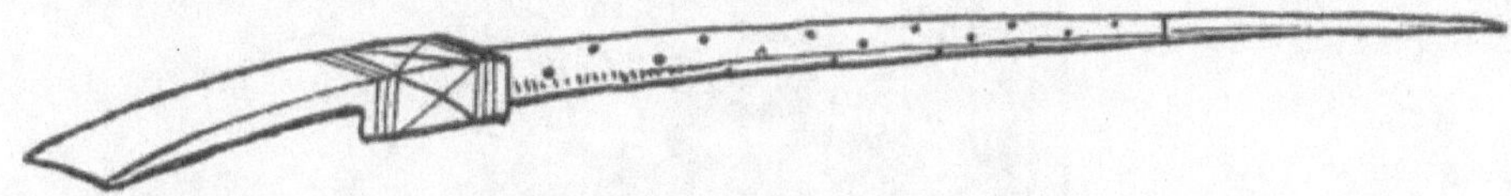

Fig. 13.—Roman diptych stylus.

Diptychs of similar form were widely used. They have been found in Egypt, and in England—remains of the Roman occupation—together with numbers of the styles used for writing with.

Diptychs were kept together at the back by means of metal rings or thongs of leather, run through holes made in the wood, so that they are true prototypes of our modern books both as to form and manner of keeping together, the "stabbed" form of binding, that is to say, threads or bands or wires run through holes pierced along the back edge of the sections of a book, having been in continual use ever since rolls were first turned into books.

When the diptychs were used as private letters they were further fastened with a tie or clasp in front, and this tie was often sealed with the sender's signet in wax or clay.

The Pompeian and all the other small wooden diptychs are unornamented, but at a later period, particularly from the second to the seventh century, Roman diptychs became of much importance and were often decoratively treated, being made of ivory and elaborately carved.

Labarte, Gori, Westwood and Maskell have all written valuable works concerning these ornamental diptychs, and specimens of more or less excellence can be found in most museums that have any collection of carvings in ivory. The earlier examples are the best; later specimens rapidly decline in art value, although they are always of great historical interest.

One leaf of one of the finest diptychs in existence is fortunately in the British Museum; it shows a full-length figure of an archangel with globe, cross and long-staff, and is supposed to have been made in the third or fourth century. A curious point about this leaf is its unusual size, about 16 by 6 inches, and it is said that such a piece could not be cut from any known elephant tusk. It is possibly mammoth ivory.

Fig. 14.—Byzantine diptych of ivory.

For a long time the supreme power at Rome was vested in the consuls who held office for one year. Naturally anyone elected to this high position was anxious to inform everyone holding any high place or office of his accession to the dignity, and the usual way of doing this was to send round diptychs of ivory announcing the event, as well as subsequent ones concerning any other important matters which might occur during the consulate.

Not only was the communication inscribed upon the wax, all of which is now gone, but the outside ivory was carved with invaluable portraits, scenes and inscriptions. By examining these carvings we can frequently ascertain who was the consul that issued them, and often enough we can find his portrait carefully drawn. In one of the many excavations made in the Forum at Rome, tablets containing a list of Roman consuls were found, and these serve as an official check upon our interpretation of the records existing upon the consular diptychs.

Fig. 15.—Ivory diptych, of the consul Valentinian, A.D. 380.

Consular diptychs were generally larger than the wooden pugillaria, which were always small. Ivory diptychs are rarely less than six or seven inches in length.

The privilege of giving away finely carved ivory diptychs was highly esteemed, and in the fourth century the Emperor Theodosius issued an edict forbidding any but one of the two consuls, one at Rome and the other at Constantinople, to issue them.

In the matter of consular and official costume the Roman carved ivory diptychs are of great importance.

Figures often appear on coins or gems, but they are always very small. On the diptychs, however, they are sufficiently large to show full details. The subjects depicted on them are various. There are games, combats in the circus, scenes from the Passion, boys emptying sacks of prizes, figures of Saints, Adam and Eve, busts and portraits of consuls both in medallions and full length. The best collections of consular diptychs are to be found at Rome, Milan, Monza, Paris, Munich, Berlin, Liverpool and London.

Besides the consular there are also ecclesiastical diptychs, the majority of which were probably only diverted from their original intention and altered and adapted to a new use. The original wax was removed and new inscriptions engraved on the ivory, mostly lists of martyrs or benefactors to the particular church which had possession of the diptych.

There is one at Liège on which the names of the bishops of Tongres are written, and there is another similar one at Novara. It is probable that the liking for ivory carvings on books arose from the lead given by the ivory diptychs. Indeed in several instances the sides of ivory diptychs are actually inlaid in late bindings of MSS.

WORKS TO CONSULT.

AGLIO, A.—Antiquities of Mexico. *London*, 1830-48. (Vol. 4, at end.) (Quipus.)

BERGER.—Histoire de l'ecriture dans l'antiquité. *Paris*, 1891.

GORI, A. F.—Thesaurus reterum diptychorum consularium et ecclesiasticorum. *Florentiae*, 1759.

HARLAND, J.—*The Reliquary*, Jan., 1865. (Clog almanacks.)

LABARTE, J.—Histoire des Arts Industrielles au moyen age. (Diptychs.) *Paris*, 1864-66.

LACROIX, P.—Les arts au moyen age. (Diptychs.) *Paris*, 1809.

LUBBOCK, SIR J.—Prehistoric Times. *London*, 1865.

MADAN, F.—Books in Manuscript. *London*, 1893.

MASKELL, W.—Ivories Ancient and Mediæval. *London*, 1875.

MASKELL, A.—Ivories. *London*, 1904.

PLOTT, R.—Natural History of Staffordshire. (Clog almanacks.) *Oxford*, 1686.

PRESCOTT, W. H.—History of the Conquest of Peru. (Quipus.) *London*.

REINAUD.—(Description des monumens Musulmanes du cabinet de M. le Duc de Blacas.) (Indian amulets.) *Paris*, 1828.

RIVETT-CARNAC, J. H.—Prehistoric Remains in Central India. *Calcutta*.

Rivett-Carnac, J. H.—Ancient Rock Sculptures in Kamaon. *Calcutta*, 1877.

Simpson, Sir J. Y.—Archaic Sculpturings. *Edinburgh*, 1867.

Smithsonian Report, 1879, p. 389. (Wampum.)

Tavernier, J. B.—Voyages. *Paris*, 1810.

Taylor, I.—The Alphabet. *London*, 1883.

Thompson, Sir E. M.—Handbook of Greek and Roman Palæography. *London*, 1893.

Westwood, J. O.—Cat. of Fictile Ivories. *London*, 1876.

CHAPTER II.

ROLLS, BOOKS AND BOOKBINDINGS.

Rolls of papyrus and vellum—Quaternions—The sewing of books—Headbands—The rounding and backing of books—Mediæval books—Irish cumdachs—Byzantine bindings—Oriental books—Modern methods of sewing and binding.

The length of ancient rolls of vellum has often puzzled bibliophiles. Rolls of narrow breadth are found 16 or 17 feet or more in length. A learned scholar on being asked how he accounted for this extraordinary length was quite puzzled, never having realised that the roll was in one piece. The neck of the giraffe seemed the only possible solution.

Fig. 16.—Egyptian papyrus roll, with mud seals.

The writer however consulted a clever leather worker and gave him a skin measuring about 3 feet by 2, suggesting certain ways of cutting it. He produced eventually, by wetting, pulling and pinning, a beautiful roll of nearly 4 inches in breadth and 16 feet 9 inches in length.

Mediæval leather workers were no doubt more skilled and practised in this particular art than anyone now is, and the experiment showed that there is really nothing out of the way in the very long rolls which at first sight seem so surprising.

Rolls were written upon in three ways. In the oldest rolls the usual way was to write lines across the breadth of the roll, which was held upright before the reader, and unrolled from the top downwards.

A rare form of writing upon rolls is that found in the prayers written on the strips which are rolled up inside Buddhist prayer wheels. Such prayers, however, are never read, but are counted as being read through on each revolution of the wheel. Each line of manuscript runs along the entire length of the roll, which is unrolled sideways. The prayer wheels vary immensely in size, the best known being the little hand ones chiefly used in Thibet; they are variously ornamented.

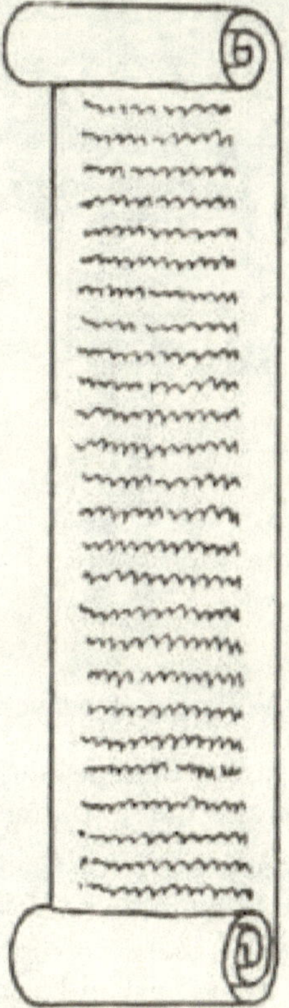

Fig. 17.—Roll written upon across its shorter diameter.

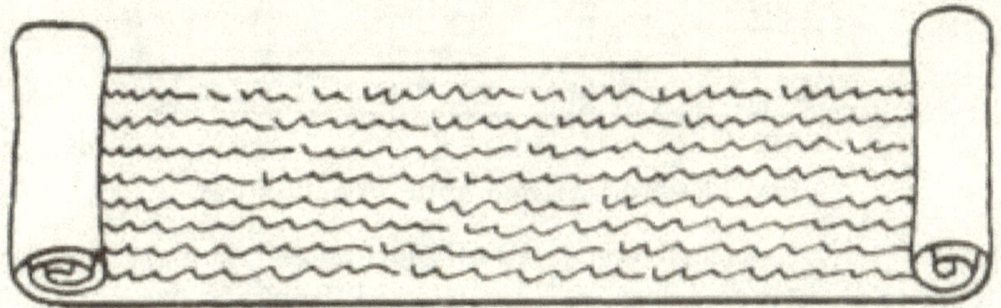

Fig. 18.—Roll written upon longitudinally.

The form of writing in rolls that is of most interest so far as books is concerned is a modification of the Thibetan form. Instead of each line running the whole length of the roll, a space limit is now fixed, and the lines of writing follow under each other, so that the page form is at once apparent. This form, a late one, can be seen in the case of the Jewish scrolls of the law. The roll is unrolled sideways, and the rollers at each end are often very handsomely decorated.

Fig. 19.—Thibetan prayer wheel.

But writing of this last kind on rolls has suggested another arrangement in which the reading is more easy, and the re-rolling of the roll itself avoided.

It will be seen that a blank space is left between each of the written "pages." Now if the vellum, bark, or paper be folded across these vacant spaces, one after the other, backwards and forwards, like accordion pleating, we shall find that we get a form of book well known in the East and also among primitive nations.

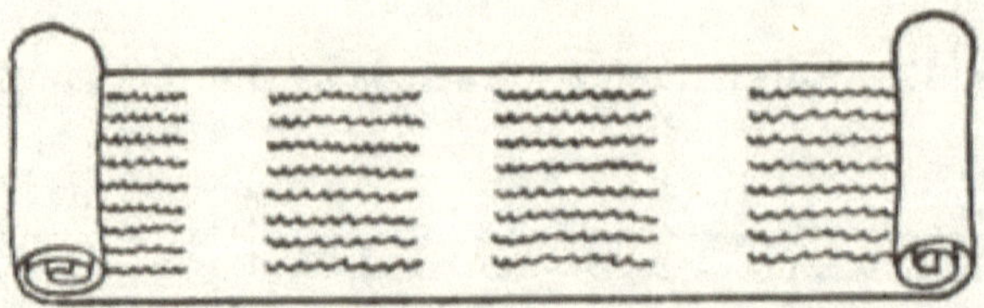

Fig. 20.—Roll written upon in page form.

Curious examples of such converted rolls can be seen in most museums, and they are generally kept flat by means of two boards front and back, but not otherwise fastened.

The Chinese and Japanese have taken this particular form of evolution from the roll to the book a step further, and by help of the ancient device of "stabbing" the flattened roll along one of its sides, they produce a form called an "Orihon," easy to consult, strong, and the blank back of the roll so hidden up that its existence is frequently not realised. But if some of the leaves of an Orihon are cut, its real structure becomes at once evident, and a book will be produced with letterpress and blank paper alternately in pairs. A similar kind of alternation shows now and then in the case of MS. rolls that have been cut up, but they are oftener arranged letterpress and blank alternately.

Fig. 21.—Sumatran bark book in the form of a folded roll.

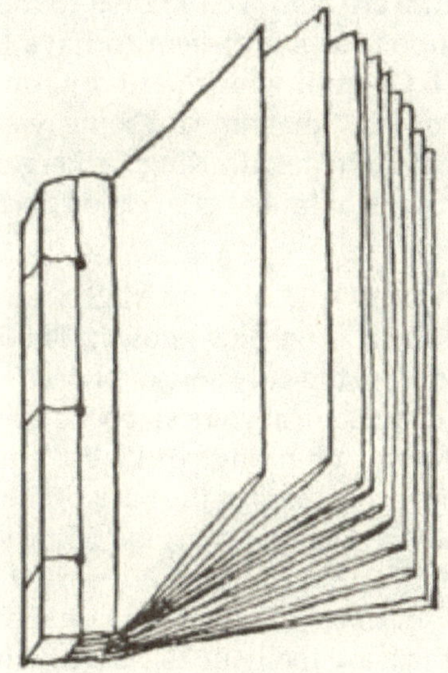

Fig. 22.—Orihon.

Without realising it we still preserve this blank and letterpress sequence, found in the converted roll, in official and legal manuscripts as well as in those intended for the printer.

When the printing press took the place of the scribe, the blank leaves had no further *raison d'être*, so they dropped out for good.

Following the rule that the forms of binding have always followed tolerably closely the forms of the manuscript they have covered, we find that rolls were kept in cylindrical boxes, called "scrinia." Each roll was usually provided with a little tag, so that if there were several of them in one box they could easily be distinguished. The same sort of tags are used to-day in the case of rolled maps kept on shelves.

Until a late period the term parchment must be understood to mean vellum. Now we call sheep skin "parchment" and calf skin "vellum," and they are prepared in the same way with lime, so that not being tanned they are not strictly "leather." The finest vellum is prepared from the very youngest and smallest calves, and it is the most beautiful and suitable material for writing or printing upon that has ever yet been found. The surface is singularly even and offers little or no resistance to a pen, so that every sort of handwriting, square or round, is put upon it with equal ease. Vellum has one fault alone, particularly when bound in book form as distinct from a roll, and this is that the edges are apt to cockle, and by so doing they not only make the pages look ugly, but they also admit the dust. Often and often magnificent vellum books, especially at the top, show large vandykes of dust-stained spaces due to this cockling, and all such books should be provided with a close fitting cardboard cap, to be kept upon them whenever they are not in use.

Parchment and vellum were both well-known to the ancients, but their value as materials for writing upon does not seem to have been fully acknowledged until the second century B.C., until which period papyrus had held undisputed pre-eminence for that purpose. At that time for some reason the supply of papyrus from Egypt ran short, and Eumenes II., King of Pergamum, successfully introduced parchment in its stead. Parchment is so called because it was first produced at Pergamum.

Until about the fifth century A.D., vellum MSS. were in the roll form, but then came a change to the book form as we now know it. This change was probably due to the fact that stabbed binding, the only sort then used, was not suited to vellum. The few papyri that exist in book form were stabbed, that is to say, the rectangular pages were kept in position by a binding cord laced through holes pierced sideways right through the entire thickness of the back of the book. The marks of these holes can often be seen along the inner margins of ancient papyri, and they also show in many instances of rebound copies of our early English printed books. To-day plenty of examples of this form of sewing can be seen in the Chinese and Japanese books, "Orihons," which are really links between the roll and the book form. It is also largely used for thin books of little value, and a modification of it can be seen in numbers of magazines, books of advertisements, and the like, which are kept together by abominable little clamps of wire attached on the same principle. When such books have to be properly bound the little clamps have to be carefully removed, and it is generally found that they have made an indelible stain of rust on the paper, even if they have not also torn it considerably.

In mediæval libraries or monasteries when a book was to be made, vellum leaves were cut into the required size and folded once across the middle. The folded leaves were then fitted inside each other in groups of four (quaternions) or five (quinternions), or whatever other number seemed good to the bookmaker. The leaves were then marked in some slight way so that their order might not be lost, and sent to the scribe to be written upon.

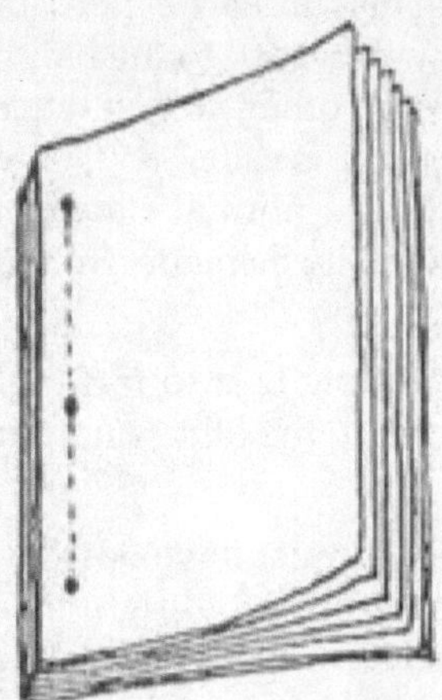

Fig. 23.—Stabbed binding.

The books count as folios because each original sheet only forms two pages; the fact of their being arranged in groups is accidental, and does not theoretically alter the size of the book. For this the original skin of vellum would have to be folded with certain further divisions, and in the case of early manuscripts this was never done.

Vellum shows a different surface on the flesh side to that on the hair side, and the scribe usually made his rule marks with a blunt style to guide his writing on the hair side, so that on this side the ruled lines are slightly indented, whereas on the flesh side they show as little ridges.

This point is apparently trivial, but if, as seems likely, both Greek and Latin scribes were really very particular and consistent in the way they alternated the two sides of the vellum, then the matter becomes one of much critical importance. Indeed, it has already been of the utmost value in deciding questions as to whether new pages had been added or not to an old book.

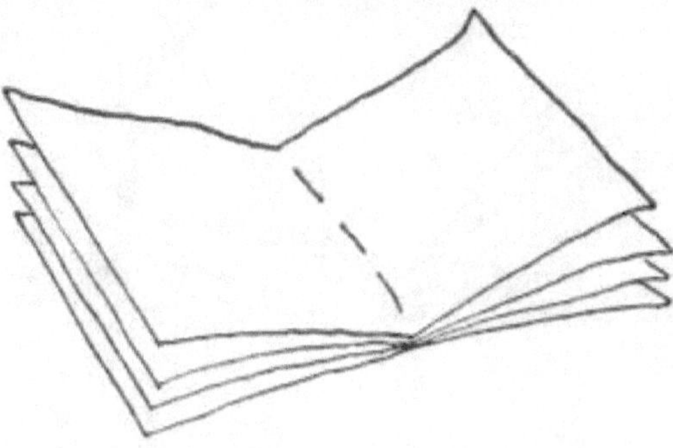

Fig. 24.—Quaternion threaded together.

When the scribe had made his rulings he then doubled up his sheets once, and arranged them as he desired with regard to the hair or flesh sides. When a section of four sheets were fitted into each other, so that when pressed together they made a solid gathering, such a gathering is called a "Quaternion," from which term we derive our word "Quire." This is a normal state of things, but it is obvious that abnormal arrangements might easily be made, from the insertion of a single leaf to that of an entirely additional section.

Now the question arose of how best to fasten the quaternions together, not only as to themselves but also as to the other quaternions, which together formed the entire book.

As to the quaternion itself, it must have been evident at once that a stitch of thread or fibre run from the innermost fold right through to the outermost would hold the leaves firmly together. It is likely enough that this was done separately at first, and then the binder would have looked at a small heap of such gatherings wondering how best to keep them together, and it would soon occur to any constructive mind to knot the loose ends of the threads together, or else to supply a supplementary cord or cords laid at right angles to the back of the sections on which the projecting ends of the threads might be tied or sewn.

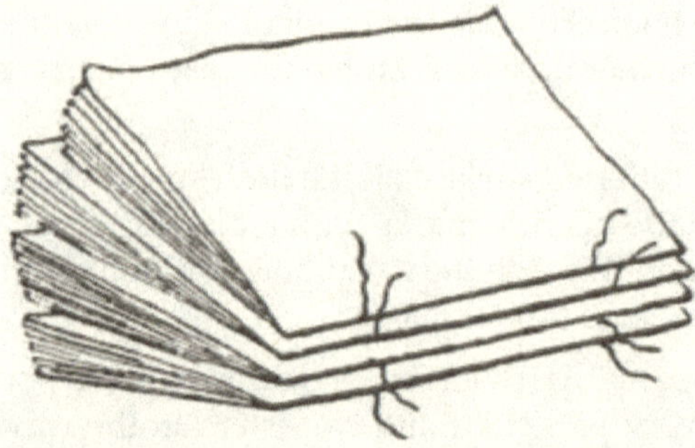

Fig. 25.—Four threaded quaternions ready to be tied together.

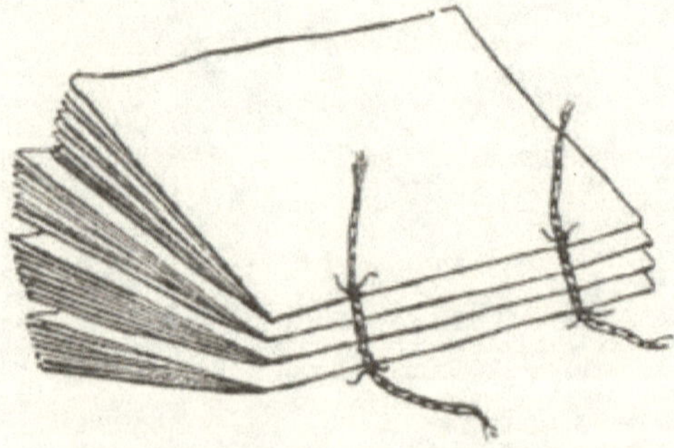

Fig. 26.—Four threaded quaternions tied on to transverse bands.

This, in fact, was done, and very shortly the best way of fastening the sections on to such cords or threads was hit upon—a method indeed that we have never bettered, and which can still be found in the work of many of our best modern binders.

At first this fastening together of the sections of a book was no doubt done uncomfortably and roughly by hand, but it soon became evident that some simple device in the form of a skeleton frame might be contrived which would render the operations of sewing and binding much easier. Not only easier to execute but also giving a more regular and workmanlike result.

The earliest known sewing frames were the same as are used now. There are two strong columns of wood fixed on a broad platform, with a slot between their bases. From capital to capital extends a bar, and the strips of leather, vellum, or hempen cords which are to form the bands of the book are looped upon it, and are kept taut by means of metal keys attached to the other end, which lock into the slot at the bottom. The bands can be quite easily adjusted to any space the worker desires.

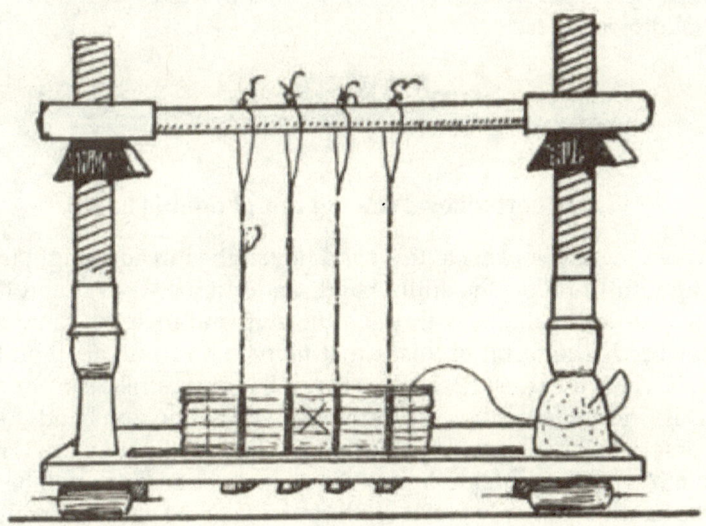

Fig. 27.—Modern hand-sewing press.

The book, ready for sewing and in proper order of sections, is laid near the worker's hand, and he, or she, takes it up by sections, one at a time. The section to be worked upon is laid downwards on the little platform, with its back close against the bands, and the worker's left hand keeps the section open in the middle, while with the right hand a thread is drawn through the back fold, from the inside to the outside, round the band, and then back from the outside to the inside, and so on until all the bands have been caught round. Then to end up, the thread is passed through near the extreme end of the fold and knotted, forming what is called a "kettle stitch," and from this point the whole operation is repeated, backwards, with the next section. It sounds complicated, but is not so really, and several sections could have been sewn together in the time that it has taken me to describe the sewing of one of them.

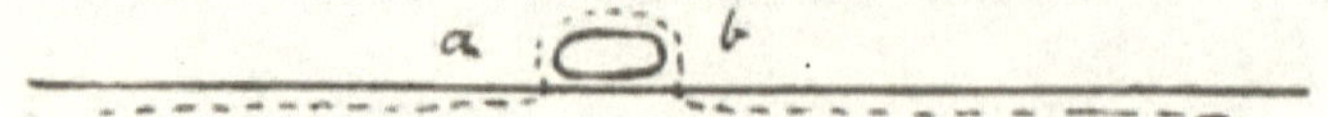

Fig. 28.—Faulty sewing over a band.

Now comes an interesting point, and that is the exact way in which the threads are passed over the bands. We will first see that if the thread is drawn through the back fold of the section, round a hand and back again through another hole, that there is a weak construction, inasmuch as the thread will have a strong tendency to cut through the paper at *a* and *b*, because there is in each case a side strain. It therefore seemed necessary that the thread should make its return journey by the same hole through which it emerged, but if simply done, this did not mend matters much, as the strain still tended to pull this hole open wider. A line of exit and entrance without any side pull was needed, and this was found by means of a very clever device. A broad band of leather or vellum was cut through lengthways, leaving a solid piece at each end.

Fig. 29.—Mediæval sewing round double band.

Now when the sewer came to this band he ran the thread straight through the slot, then brought it round the entire band, under it, between it and the back of the book, and down again, back through the slot, and in at the same point from which it emerged. The result of this is that there is no strain at all on the needle hole through which the thread passes, as the pull is quite straight both coming and going. This is undoubtedly the best form of sewing a book on bands, and a book so treated is said to be sewn on "double bands." But our recent work is not always true, although from the outside it appears correct, because in numbers of cases such double bands are simply glued on the outside of the back, the real sewing, of a very inferior kind, possibly even done by machinery, being hidden underneath the leather. Few great binders except Charles Lewis have ever used sham bands.

Flexible sewn books can be had now if wanted, but the sewing on the bands is not quite the same as the fine mediæval double bands I have described. It is, however, practically nearly as good, and the bands themselves can be made smaller.

Fig. 30.—Modern sewing round single band.

The modern method is to bring the needle and thread through the back of the section as usual, then give it one turn onwards over the band and back again through the same hole. It will be seen that this is a thoroughly sound principle, and brings no strain upon the back of the section.

The ends of the bands of limp vellum books have always been treated in the same way; they are drawn straight through the vellum at the joint and then back again and fastened inside by means of the end paper.

The manner of drawing the bands of a "limp" vellum bound book through the limp vellum cover is of much interest, and it survives in many instances where boards are used.

In principle it is the same process as is described further on with regard to boarded books, but in the case of the limp vellum bindings the ends of the bands are normally visible for a short length, but in the case of boarded books they are always covered up with the exception of some vellum-covered boarded books in which the limp vellum peculiarity is preserved.

Another small point of interest about the old limp vellum bindings is that the head and tail bands are made of the same sort of thin vellum strip as the main bands and carefully drawn diagonally through the vellum at the corners and fastened inside. Dealt with in this way the head band becomes of real structural value, much of which is lost if it is cut off short as is done in the large majority of cases.

William Morris liked limp vellum bindings and often used them, but without head bands. Instead of the short strips of vellum used for bands in old books Morris used specially prepared silk tapes, and brought them through the vellum at the joint in the old-fashioned way. Instead of being cut short and pasted down as the old limp vellum bands were, Morris continued his tapes and brought them out again near the front edge of the vellum, where they could be tied. This is an excellent arrangement and keeps such a book together in an admirable and effective way.

Vellum bindings required flat backs because the material would not yield sufficiently to be tucked round the projecting bands of a normal flexible bound book, in which the leather back is firmly fixed over the bands. Nevertheless in several instances old vellum books, in boards, which have been sewn on raised bands show traces of these bands in low relief across the back. In such cases it is common to find that some padding has been put in the spaces between the bands so as to level the back up. Books treated in this way are usually stiff to open and uncomfortable to consult.

The flat back, which was necessary for the same reason in the case of books bound at a later date in velvet, cloth, silk or canvas, necessitated some modification of the thick projecting bands of the ordinary book, and the requisite flatness was attained by using strips of vellum or tape instead of cords of hemp. Then it was found that it was not necessary to fasten the back of the cover to the back of the sections, so the "hollow back" came into existence.

The majority of modern books are bound with hollow backs; it can be recognised by opening a book to the full and seeing if the back is separate, and it has one real virtue as well as several vices. If a book should happen to be printed too far back, a hollow back binding will enable it to "throw up," and show the printing right down to the inner edge of the paper, whereas a flexible binding always tends to open less freely, especially in the middle.

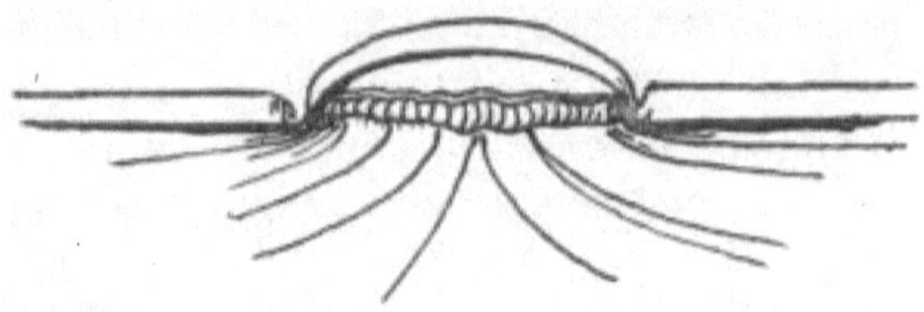

Fig. 31.—Book bound with "open" or "hollow" back, and modern headband, cut off at each end.

For books that are likely to be much used hollow backs are unadvisable as they are sooner worn out, but for small light books there is no doubt much to be said in their favour.

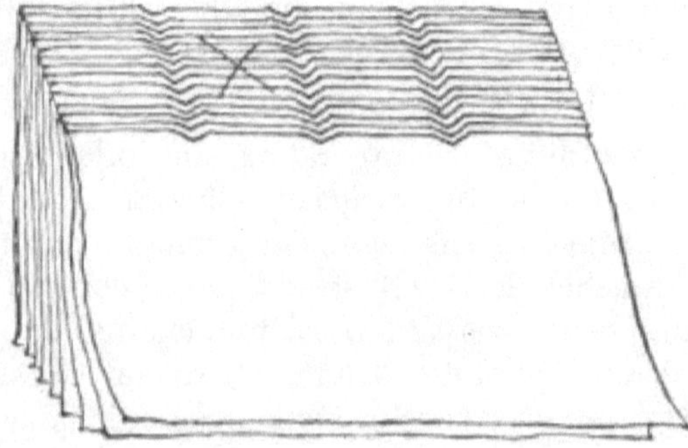

Fig. 32.—Back of book prepared with cut trenches to hold the bands.

Among English binders of note I think Charles Lewis was the first to use hollow backs extensively. But for fine books there is no doubt that the old-fashioned flexible sewing on raised bands is the best in the long run. Books bound with hollow backs often have the bands "sawn in," that is to say, a trench is cut for each band across the back of the sections. In these trenches the bands are laid, and the sewing is of a simpler and quicker sort than it is when the thread is brought round each band as it is in the flexible style. Moreover, there is a weak point where the thread touches the edge of the saw cut, and at this place the paper is always apt to give. It is obvious that to cut away paper from the back of a section must always be not only a barbarism but also structurally wrong. Such a method of sewing a book can only be excused on the score of cheapness, and it may be urged that in this case it does not matter.

Towards the end of the fifteenth century it was found that the extreme tops and bottoms of the backs of the sections of bound books not only looked untidy and unfinished, but also that they tended to gape, in fact they were weak points both structurally and artistically. When it was once realised it was soon rectified, and a small additional band was made of a strip of leather or vellum, to fit along the outer edge of the top and bottom at the back. This slip was then sewn on by means of thread and button-hole stitching, being caught in at intervals by a long stitch drawn through the centre of one or other of the sections of the book. The loose ends of the headband itself were drawn in to the boards, forming in fact an additional band. The headband is a point in the forwarding of a book which has not received much notice as yet, but it is of some importance, as there is no doubt that much attention has been paid by binders to the ornamentation of headbands from mediæval times until now, and it is the first point in the binding of a book in which ornament is considered.

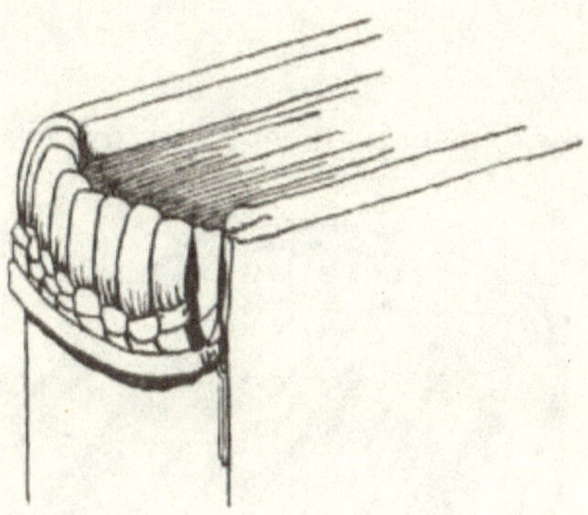

Fig. 33.—French sixteenth century headband.

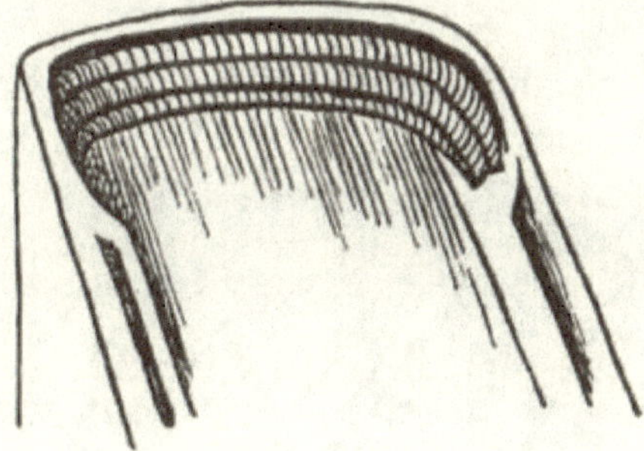

Fig. 34.—Italian fifteenth century headband.

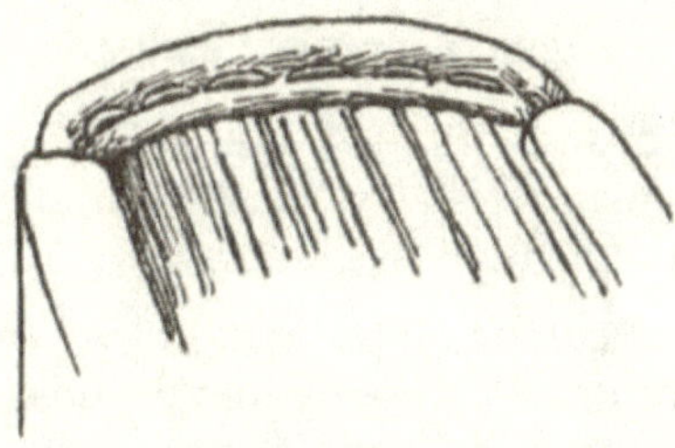

Fig. 35.—German fifteenth century headband.

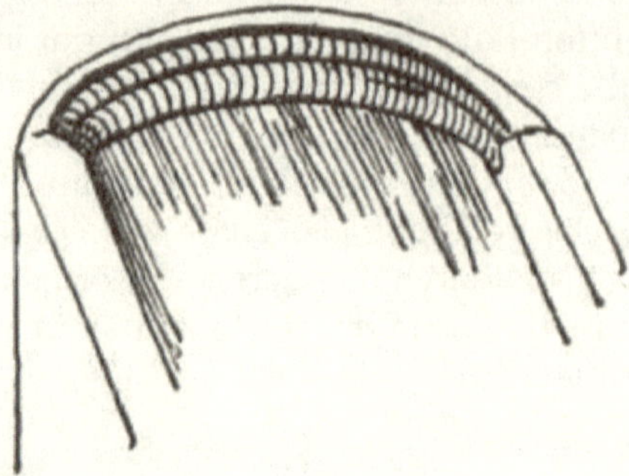

Fig. 36.—English seventeenth century headband.

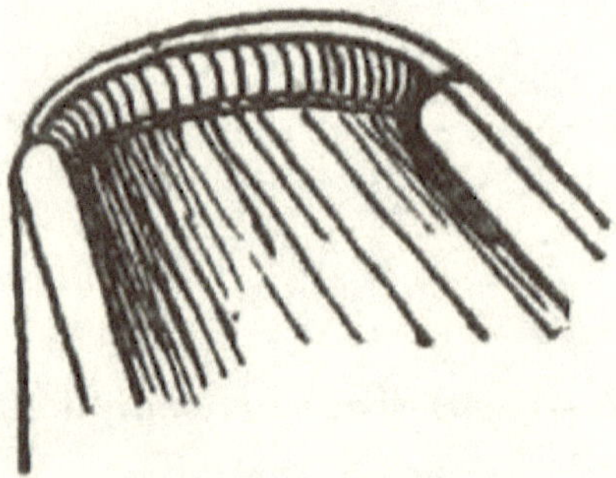

Fig. 37.—English eighteenth century headband, by Roger Payne.

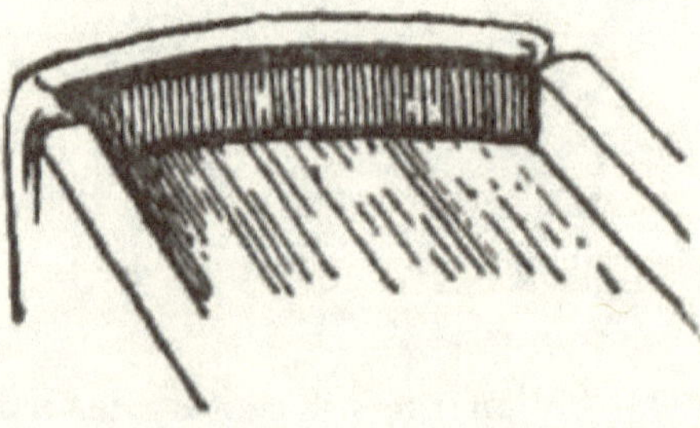

Fig. 38.—English nineteenth century headband, by Charles Lewis.

Some of the early headbands are sewn over with strips of soft leather, and at a later time they are cut in distinctive ways, flat or round, and sewn over with silks of particular colours or combinations of colours.

Of late years the vice of cutting off the ends of the headband has come into being; these ends ought to be drawn properly into the boards, as Mr. Douglas Cockerell has indeed done for me in several instances. But no words can adequately condemn the miserable ready-made coloured slips which are often found simply *stuck on* in the proper place.

Fig. 39.—What a book may do if the back is not properly rounded.

Vellum books were the first to be properly bound. The papyri which were stabbed are so rare that they may be passed by. As I have already said, vellum is apt to be curly; for this reason the boards used for binding in early days were made of thick wood, the heaviness of which, even when unaided by clasps, tended to keep the vellum flat.

Fig. 40.—Book with flat back.

Beech wood was largely used for these old covers, and from the German word "Buch," meaning beech, we derive our word "book." Beechen boards were light, decorative, and very carefully dried and seasoned. It is remarkable how flat such old boards are, and they were no doubt very highly valued as they often have upon them the stamp of the monastery in which they were used.

The edges of the boards are sometimes bevelled, from the upper side in English or French books, and from the under side in German books—but such a distinction must not be taken as invariable. Boards often show signs of having been used more than once, and it is rarely that any decoration shows on the wood. In a few cases of German books may be found outline drawings of an heraldic nature.

Fig. 41.—Book with flat back falling in.

The first bound books were made with flat backs, and the boards fitted close upon the outer sheets of vellum, papyrus or paper. In this formation, however, it was found that there was a strong liability for the back to fall in and the foredge to project outwards.

As early as the fifteenth century, in the case of printed books on paper, this fault of the back falling in led some few binders to neutralise it by giving the back of the book a rounded form by means of hammering, and this quite prevented the falling in of the back. The exact extent of the rounding can easily be seen by looking at the front edge of a book, because the curves of the back and front correspond. The boards, however, remained in their first position, flat on the outer sheets.

Fig. 42.—Book with rounded back.

But another trouble was apparent in both these cases, namely, that when such books were opened, the joint between the boards and the back showed a tendency to pull up the few pages next adjacent. In time these pages became torn and injured, and constructively there was something wrong with the principle of attachment.

Paper is soft, and when a "rounded" book was fitted with hard boards and strongly pressed there would be a certain tendency for the boards to sink into the mass of the paper and to throw up a small ridge along the edge of the back. Such a small accidental ridge is often found on old paper books.

Fig. 43.—Book with back rounded and backed.

But there is no doubt that the actual process of making an intentional groove for the boards to fit in was practised by a few fifteenth century binders in England. This groove is made by an extension of the process of rounding the back, and it is produced by hammering the back over two hard boards carefully placed in the proper position. The shape of a back thus treated is theoretically as shown in Fig. 44, and it will be seen that the actual joint now falls away from the body of the book and is removed to the artificial line along the outer edge of the groove, and from this line the projecting bands are drawn in to the boards. If this operation of "backing" is properly done it is almost impossible for the back of a book to fall in. It will always open easily and return to its original form, and if the bands are properly attached to the boards, the latter will never fall off.

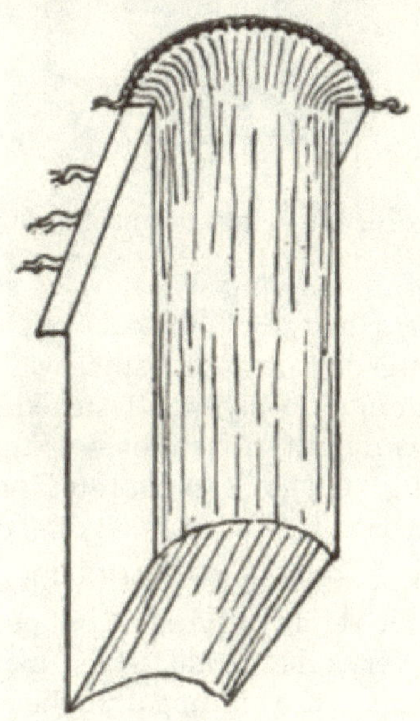

Fig. 44.—Book rounded and backed, before the boards are put on.

Although the principle of backing was known at the early time mentioned, it was not universally understood and practised until quite recent times. Now, however, it is fully recognised as one of the most important processes in the binding of books, especially large ones.

We have seen that the book sewn in leather bands has the ends of these bands left loose, projecting in the case of a large book some two or three inches. Holes were now carefully cut along the back edge of the board to fit the ends of the bands, sloping upwards, and some little way in other slots were cut from the upper surface of the board to meet them. Into these holes the ends of the bands were drawn, and when in proper position they were pegged down with one or more small wooden pegs. Sometimes the bands were drawn right through the boards and fastened inside. Numbers and numbers of instances of this work exist and are quite sound to-day. But such books do not open satisfactorily, as there is a disagreeable pull upon the outer sections when the book is opened. In fact, the junction between the bands and the boards is not scientifically correct, because the backs are not rounded.

Fig. 45.—Half-bound book.

The vulnerable part of the binding will now be seen to be the soft threads which cover the bands where they adjoin the back of the sections of the book, and to protect these delicate threads a strip of leather was cut, damped and pressed over the bands so as to fit quite closely, and fastened on with glue, projecting a short way over on to the board itself so as to cover up the holes used for the bands. This is called a "half-binding." On the leather of such half-bindings there is usually some blind tooling, lines or rolls or even small cameo stamps.

Mediæval bindings are commonly provided with clasps. The original reason of this was to help to keep the vellum leaves flat, but of course artistic binders saw that clasps might be made very ornamental, and so many of them are. They have survived as ornamental adjuncts to a binding until the present day, although there is no necessity for them.

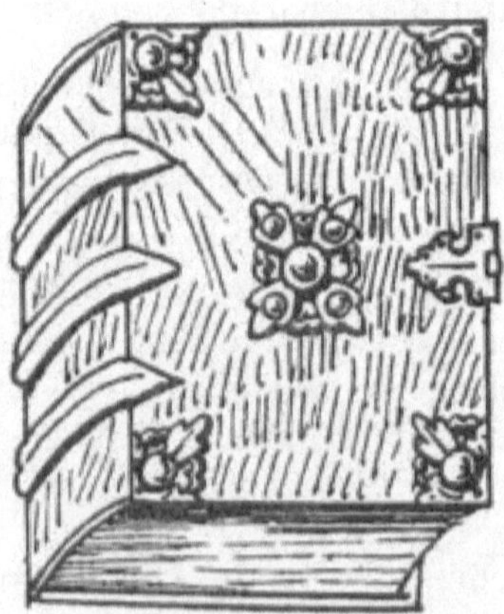

Fig. 46.—Mediæval book with bosses, corner pieces and clasps.

Bosses in the centre and at the corners of mediæval bindings were of structural use, as they protected the actual boards of the book from wear. In early days books were kept upon their sides and probably had flat boards between each volume. So the bosses took the wear and preserved the books. Many of the mediæval bosses and corners have ornamental settings; they are generally of brass, but sometimes of silver or wood. The titles of such books were sometimes written on the front edges and sometimes on a slip of paper fastened under horn on the upper board, and in the late fifteenth century they were sometimes lettered in gold or blind, also on the boards.

It happened that the art of Byzantium was in its prime just about the same time that vellum began to be arranged in sections—in book form—in contradistinction to the roll form. So we find some of the finest examples of Byzantine art on bookbindings. Of course it must be understood that these richly worked covers are only ornamentally added to the true binding underneath, and the actual work of the binding is more or less as I have already described it. But the decorative art in these cases is so predominant that they are generically known as "Byzantine" bindings.

Fig. 47.—German binding of about the eleventh century,
with cabochon crystals.

The large majority of the known specimens of this kind are no longer in company with their original manuscripts. Many of them are preserved simply as loose covers, and alien manuscripts have been inserted in others. I expect that there are still considerable numbers of these bindings preserved in remote churches and monasteries in Central Europe, and some day perhaps some traveller with sufficient knowledge and time at his command will make search for them. But for the present fine and genuine examples of Byzantine bindings are of great rarity. It is said that there are not more than about three hundred of them known. The life history of many of these is well known, and so are many of the additions and alterations to which they have been subjected during their long life. Luckily some of the finest are now safely housed in our London museums, and others are, or are likely to be, safe in a great local museum.

To be able to judge whether these bindings are genuine, a librarian must be an antiquary, a goldsmith and silversmith, skilled both in repoussé work, engraving and cast work, a gem cutter, an enameller, a skilled bookbinder, and an artist, and if he fails in one of these knowledges his judgment cannot be relied on. An ordinary art critic who possesses "Flaire" can pick up a certain amount of knowledge by reason of having made many mistakes and profited by them, and if he has been fortunately able to associate himself only with true and known fine examples for a long time, he may eventually be a good guesser. But no true judgment can be given without actual technical knowledge.

Fig. 48.—**French binding of the thirteenth century with enamels.**

The result of all this is, that collectors of such bindings have been freely victimised. It is not really difficult to copy or to imitate a Byzantine binding—it is not nearly so difficult as to counterfeit a fine Le Gascon or a fine Roger Payne. It does not so much concern the binder as the metal worker, and in metal a little skill goes a long way, and so it does in the cloisonne enamel work which alone is found in these bindings. The present market price of a very fine Byzantine binding—a known one—will run into five figures, so it is little to be wondered at that it pays the clever *faussaires* of the Continent to direct their attention to covers of this kind. They need not even take the trouble to provide manuscripts for the inside; loose covers will sell with equal readiness.

Ivory carving played an important part on early bindings. Apart from diptychs, the earliest known decorative binding consists of plaques of ivory carved with Biblical scenes, and having in the centre a lamb within a wreath of cloisonne work, with inlays of coloured glass. It is now kept in the cathedral treasury at Milan, and is without its original inside; it is attributed to the fifth century.

Early Irish manuscripts were usually bound in quite simple limp leather covers, but these were kept in book boxes or "Cumdachs," all of which still existing are of the greatest interest.

Fig. 49.—The upper cover of the Cumdach of the Stowe Missal.

One of the finest is that of the Stowe Missal, dating from about the eleventh century. It belonged originally to the monastery of Lorrha in Tipperary, whence it was taken to the Irish monastery of Ratisbon. In 1784 it was found by Mr. John Grace in Austria, and afterwards belonged to the Stowe Library, and Lord Ashburnham, from whom it was purchased by the nation in 1883 with the rest of his library, and then deposited in the museum of the Royal Irish Academy.

The lid is ornamented with a large cross set with pearls and metal bosses, having in the centre a large oval crystal over a pink ground, and enclosed with recent enamels, no doubt replacing old ones. At each end of the cross is a large jewel. The spaces between the arms of the cross contain silver gilt plates engraved with figures of Saints, and on the silver edge plates is an inscription in Irish inviting the reader to "Pray for Dunchad descendant of Taccan of the family of Cluan who made this." This may therefore be called the earliest signed binding in the world, if a cumdach can be considered a binding. No doubt much of the work now on this lid, as well as some of the jewels and their settings, have been added since the original work was made.

The base of the box has a similar ornamentation upon it, but the jewels and enamels are all gone, the spaces between the arms of the cross being filled with silver plates cut into an open pattern set over bronze gilt.

The sides of the box are much destroyed, but they have fortunately not been restored. The ornamentation consists of enamelled bosses or curious castings in the centre of each side, flanked by panels of open designs cut out of thin silver over gilt, and corner ornaments of cast work. There are small bosses of blue enamel.

The remarkable open work over gilt bronze occurs again in the base of the cumdach containing Molaise gospels, it also belongs to the eleventh century, and this sort of ornamentation seems to be characteristic of Irish work of that time. The lid of the box is ornamented in a modification of the same idea, but in this case the bronze showing through the silver is beautifully worked. The main idea is a cross, and between the arms are the evangelistic emblems, and with their names, Leo, Aquila, Homo, Taurus. An inscription asks us to "Pray for Cenn, for the successor of Molaise for whom this case was made by Gillabaithain the artisan." It is possible that this may be a little earlier than the Stowe cumdach.

A few more cumdachs are known, about ten of them altogether, and others are recorded only.

There is that of Dimma's book, of the Cathach of the O'Donnells, and several others, some of which are quite plain.

Other book cases were made of beautifully worked leather. The satchel of the Book of Armagh is one of these, and leather cases or "Forels" were made of cuirbouilli in the fifteenth and sixteenth centuries, particularly in Italy. These forels were in the shape now known as "slip off" cases, and they generally had attachments for a strap. They are always charmingly chased, and often bear heraldic ornamentation.

Cuirbouilli was calf or hide, worked with knife, style, or hammer, and then probably boiled in oil, but the exact process that was used is now unknown. It is very strong, and its value was known in England, where it was used to make wrist guards for archery, but as far as I know it was never used here for bindings or covers for bindings. I have heard the calf or sheep bindings of the early sixteenth century, bearing panel stamps, described as cuirbouilli, but they are not so.

The earliest cover still containing its original manuscript is probably that given with other treasure to Theodelinda, Queen of the Lombards, by Pope Gregory the Great, in the seventh century. It is now kept in the cathedral treasury at Monza.

The manuscript is described in a contemporary document as being "theca persica inclusam," and, so far, its cover resembles the Irish cumdachs. The case is of gold, ornamented with a large cross, outlined with lines of small flat garnets, with sapphires and emeralds, set in cloisons. The body of the cross is richly jewelled with cabochon cut stones and pearls, and at the extremity of each arm is a curious glass bead of millefiori glass, green with a little red flower in the centre.

Between the arms of the cross are four gamma shaped ornaments, each set with small flat jewels. Across the sides are bands of gold on which are engraved the words De Donis Dei offerit Theodelenda reg. gloriosissima sancto Joanni Baptiste in Basilica quem ipsa fundavit in Modicia prope palatium suum. A handsome border with flat garnets enclosed the whole, and the four cameos set near the gammas are a recent addition. Byzantine art is generally considered as a decadent form of Roman art, but in this particular instance there is much Greek feeling, and it is in all respects, excepting perhaps the inscription, a magnificent piece of work.

Fig. 50.—The binding of the Gospels of Lindau, the older side.

The binding of the Gospels of Lindau has now two sides of different dates, each of which has been repaired and added to in recent times. The earlier of the two, far the finer, is probably contemporary with the manuscript, having been made about the later half of the ninth century, as the Abbey of the Noble Canonesses at Lindau was founded by the Emperor Lewis the Pious in A.D. 834. A large golden cross pattée is the chief motive of this beautiful piece of work, and it is ornamented with rare enamels showing bust figures wearing stoles, and jewels in great variety, the borderings being inlaid with small flat pieces of garnet. The spaces between the arms of the cross are filled with bronze plaques elaborately ornamented with Celtic interlacings in chiselled work. The workmanship is probably Irish, and was most likely done abroad, possibly enough at Lindau itself, by some Irish artists who had emigrated. Irish jewellers and enamellers of this early time were justly celebrated, and their services were secured whenever possible.

The later side of the binding is one of the finest existing specimens of Carlovingian art. It is radically different from the earlier side and was probably added about the eleventh or twelfth century.

Fig. 51.—The binding of the Gospels of Lindau, the more recent side.

In the centre is a large cross on which is a gilt figure of our Lord in the attitude of the crucifixion. The cross is outlined by a structure of open work of gold ornamented with filagree work and thickly set with jewels. Between the arms of the cross are angels worked in repoussé, and rich bosses of gold and jewels, raised on arcades of open work. The border is of great richness, and is thickly sown with large jewels cut "en cabochon," many of them pierced longitudinally, betraying in all probability an Oriental provenance. No doubt this was originally made for some valuable manuscript now lost, and it was used to replace the original simple lower cover of the Gospels of Lindau at some unknown time.

The book was formerly in the possession of the Earl of Ashburnham, but now it is gone to America.

Beautiful Byzantine work of the twelfth century is to be seen upon the carved and jewelled binding of the Psalter of Melissenda, daughter of Baldwin II., King of Jerusalem, and wife of Fulk, his successor. The ivory covers measure eight by six inches, and are elaborately carved in bas relief with Biblical scenes. On each side are six circles, and in each circle a little figure group, on one side representing episodes in the life of David and on the other works of mercy. There is lettering run in with red, giving the names of each of the personages shown, and their eyes are set with tiny rubies or emeralds cut "en cabochon" like coloured grains of sand. The spaces between the circles are filled with other Biblical or symbolical figures, scrolls and animals, and a beautiful interlacing border encloses the whole, set with turquoises and rubies.

The carver's name, "HERODIUS," is cut in the lower cover. The workmanship on these ivories is extremely fine, and there is no doubt they were made to be used as a binding. The majority of ivory carvings found on mediæval bookbindings appear to have been simply added, having been originally made for some other purpose. But there are notable exceptions, particularly in the Bibliothèque Nationale at Paris. The shape in which the plaque of ivory is cut will often give a valuable indication in this matter.

The finest Byzantine binding now in England is probably that known as the Gospels of Charlemagne, now in the Victoria and Albert Museum. It is nearly square, and the upper side is overlaid with gilt metal, enamels and gems. In the centre is a seated figure of Our Lord in the attitude of Benediction, in repoussé work. Round this is a band of white and green enamelled lettering, restored, on which are two hexameter lines: "MATHEVS ET MARCVS LVCAS SCSQ JOHANE VOX HORV QVATVOR REBOAT TE XPE REDEMPTOR." The outer border is made up of rectangular plaques of enamels, gold work and jewels.

The work here is also largely restored, but it is, as a rule, admirably done, and where the old work remains, especially in the gold, it is of a high excellence. The jewels have, for the most part, been restored. As the book is now it is a splendid and dignified example of its kind; the under side is simply covered with strong red leather, with a cross marked by small studs. Like many of these splendid altar books, this one is said to have served as a Pax.

The manuscript itself is of the tenth century, and belonged to the Abbey

Church of St. Maurice d'Agaune, and from here it was stolen in the fourteenth century. It afterwards found a home at Sion, and was purchased for the Victoria and Albert Museum at the Spitzer sale in 1893.

No doubt examples of rich monastic bindings did exist in England, but none of them are now known. It is likely enough that their value condemned them, and that they were entirely destroyed in the earlier half of the sixteenth century to swell the revenues of the king. The manuscripts belonging to these destroyed covers have, luckily, been kept, and numbers of them came to the British Museum by gift of George II.

Two ornamental bindings only of English origin now remain; these are both simple, they are the St. Cuthbert's Gospels and the English coronation book of Henry I. These are described in Chapter VIII.

There were plenty of leather bindings ornamented with blind tooling or cut leather work in mediæval times, and these also are described later on.

The idea of ornamenting bindings with sunk panels is of Arab origin. The fashion came to Europe by way of Venice, and the Venetians themselves quickly saw that the possibilities of decorating bindings were largely increased by this device. It is done by means of two boards, the upper of which is pierced, then the whole is covered with leather and ornamented with painted work or stamped work as the case may be. In inferior bindings of this sort, the sunk panels are sometimes produced simply by hard pressure, but the state of the edges of the panels will soon show how they are made. If they are steep there are the double boards, if very sloping there may only be one.

Queen Elizabeth had some of these Venetian sunk bindings presented to her and she liked them. Consequently there were a few examples of it made in England in the sixteenth century. At a later time Charles Lewis bound several large books with double boards in this way, and I think he was the only important English binder who has ever done so to any great extent.

The double boards have left a trace of their existence in the form of a trench which is frequently found along the edges of the boards of sixteenth century bindings of English, Italian, and French workmanship. The trench, however, is merely a survival and does not necessarily imply the actual existence of double boards. It is a distant tribute to our indebtedness to the East.

In some of the double-board books bound for Queen Elizabeth, with sunk panels, the headband is curiously produced away from its normal finishing point and is carried right round the entire edge of the boards in the trench between the boards. It is a decorative and curious peculiarity, and I have never met with it in any foreign books.

Wooden boards were used for bindings until about the end of the fifteenth century, when the idea of using several layers of paper pasted together—paste boards—was thought of. In fact, paste boards may be considered to have been introduced about the same time as printing, and waste printed matter was often used for making them with.

There are many instances in which valuable printed matter has been found hidden up in binder's boards, and as these can generally be soaked apart and cleaned, we already owe the preservation of several unique fragments to the fact of their having been used for bindings.

Fig. 52.—Painted Persian binding (Nadir Shah at the battle of Karnul).

Persian manuscripts of the seventeenth to the nineteenth centuries are often ornamented in a manner which is of considerable interest. They are bound in paste boards like all other Oriental bindings known to me, and are covered with some sort of gesso applied in a thin layer. On this gesso are paintings of varied merit; some of them, especially the historical and hunting scenes, are extremely well done, and others, mostly floral, are of a commonplace character. The boards are sometimes painted inside and out.

The painting is done in water-colours, and is of the same sort as is found with the manuscript inside, but generally by an inferior artist. When finished the painting was thickly varnished, and this varnish has darkened by time into a mellow golden colour which improves the appearance of the colour work underneath.

The darkening of this varnish has, however, had a remarkable result: the photographic ray cannot pierce it except here and there—in fact, the painting is covered by a non-actinic curtain. A photograph will only show the surface of the varnish with here and there a patch where the blue colour underneath succeeds in making itself felt.

Ornamental though these painted and varnished bindings are, there is unfortunately a great and inherent delicacy about them, and it is that the varnished surface is badly given to chipping off. It is difficult to say what the best remedy for this chipping or flaking off is; it is probably due to the discrepancy in hardness between the hard varnish and the soft boards; it seems to be radical.

Experiments are needed in this matter, but owners of fine specimens, even if chipped, are naturally chary of allowing experiments which may do harm as well as good. I should say that probably much good might be done by dropping a little collodion so as to make it run down between the loosened surfaces; it will act as a cement and strengthen as well as fasten them together. It is also likely that thin glue applied several times might also do good used in the same way, but I believe collodion is better and penetrates weak places more readily.

The same styles of ornamentation are used on mirror cases and other small objects, so that although many bindings are so treated, yet the method is not one exclusively used for such purpose. But no doubt the finest work was put on bindings, some of which are large.

Another Persian manner is that of using large metal stamps impressed with elaborate arabesques. The impressions from these stamps of course give a design in relief. The whole impression is generally gilded in various tints, and the small design itself is often picked out with a little colour. Many of these arabesque panel stamps are of wonderful beauty.

Arabic and other Oriental bindings have a curious flap projecting from one of the boards, which covers and protects the front edges. The flaps are ornamented in the same way as the rest of the binding.

The sewing and the paper of all these books is weak and light, but there is always work of much interest on the bindings. The backs are flat and the paste boards are thin and covered with very thin leather. They are usually ornamented inside and outside with blind and gilt work, stamped and cut work, and hand painting, in much variety.

Fig. 53.—Oriental binding with flap.

The open work cut with a knife from thin leather is remarkable for its extraordinary precision and delicacy; it is usually in arabesques with small flowers, and often coloured by hand. It is always set on a background of colour, either painted or a bit of coloured paper. But the work is very frail, and panels of it are rarely found perfect.

Oriental bindings are altogether weak, and they will not stand hard wear.

Now we have, chiefly from America, machines that will do almost every one of the hand-operations for binding a book. There are sewing machines that only want to be fed with thread and the books to be sewn; there are casing machines of wonderful speed and accuracy, backing machines and binding machines. The only one thing that cannot yet be done by a machine is the pasting down the ends of the bands or tapes inside the boards. I rather think that many of these machines strain the paper badly, and also they require setting elaborately to a certain size. They are very useful for large, cheap editions, but little use for good miscellaneous work. Nothing is really so good as the old-fashioned sewing on raised bands by hand.

BOOKS TO CONSULT.

COCKERELL, D. Bookbinding. *London*, 1901.

DAVENPORT, C. Cantor Lectures on Decorative Bookbinding. *London*, 1898.

DAVENPORT, C. (Encyc. Brit. Article Bookbinding). *London*, 1902.

DU SOMMERARD, A. Les arts au Moyen Age. *Paris*, 1838-46.

GORI, A. F. Thesaurus vet. Diptychorum. *Florentiæ*, 1759.

LABARTE, J. Hist. des Arts au Moyen Age. *Paris*, 1864.

LIBRI, COUNT G. Catalogue. *Paris*, 1857.

MADAN, F. Books in Manuscript. *London*, 1893.

CHAPTER III.

PAPER.

Paper—Watermarks—Quiring.

Although we get our word "paper" from "papyrus," this latter was not a paper at all. The essential characteristic of a true paper is the matting or felting together of small fibres, whether these be of wood, linen, or other substance. Papyrus was the inner bark of a beautiful reed, which grows along the banks of the Nile, and from a very remote period strips of this bark were laid over each other at right angles, fixed together with gum, or perhaps a little Nile mud, and used for writing upon with a soft pen. The right-angular lines of the two layers of papyrus bark can easily be seen on any papyrus MS.

Papyrus is not a good substance for writing upon; it is at first too soft, and then it gets brittle and is apt to crumble away. By sticking successive strips of papyrus to each other ancient scribes produced long rolls of manuscript, and from these rolls we derive many of the book terms which are still in use. The most obvious is "volume," which is from "volvere," "to roll up"; and "Bible" comes from the Greek "βυβλοί," meaning the inner bark of papyrus.

In China the possibility of making thin feltings with silk fibre was probably known at a very remote period, and it is likely enough that from some such unsatisfactory production the better and usable kinds made of vegetable fibres evolved itself. We cannot now say when the possibility of felting together fibres of wood or grass first became known to the Chinese, but it was certainly well understood in the fifth or sixth centuries, because specimens of it still exist.

In the middle of the eighth century, in 751 A.D., there were certain tribal disturbances on the Chinese frontier of Persia, and one of the combatants called in the help of the Chinese. These, however, suffered defeat at the hands of the Arab governor of Samarkand, who brought back some Chinese prisoners to his town. These men were acquainted with the Chinese methods of making paper.

From these Chinese prisoners the Arabs and their friends the Persians learnt the art of paper-making with vegetable fibres, but the supply in this particular very soon gave out, and because enough suitable fibres were difficult to get they mixed them with pulped rags. Eventually the Samarkand paper-makers used rags only, and these they easily got in sufficient quantities from old linen clothes, and also the mummy wrappings from Egypt were made use of in the same way.

From the Arabs the knowledge of paper-making passed rapidly to Europe, and by the middle of the tenth century it had entirely superseded the use of papyrus.

The researches of Dr. J. Wiesner and Dr. J. Karabacek, both professors of the University of Vienna, have been of incalculable value as regards the composition and history of ancient paper, and they were fortunate enough to have the opportunity of examining the papers in the collection of the Archduke Rainer, among which are specimens of very early work. The professors have examined these and other old papers microscopically and chemically, and found that from the beginning it was considered necessary to load papers with some binding or filling substance; they found starch, starch flour, probably from rice, and among the Chinese papers a dressing of powdered gypsum. Without some such dressing the papers would have resembled our blotting paper, and it would have been almost impossible to write upon them.

Professor Wiesner found that Chinese papers of the eighth century were really mixed papers; they contained fibres of mulberry bark, hemp and rags. Rags of fishing nets themselves would contain fibres of flax, hemp, and China grass. But the main constituent of ancient Chinese paper is fibre of mulberry-bark, and I believe it is so still, although China grass fibre is also much used.

Specimens of Chinese papers from the eighth century onwards can be seen at the British Museum. They are soft, but have lasted fairly well, and do not appear to show any wire marks. The colour of these papers is much the same as Chinese papers made now, but in some instances they have certainly darkened as modern wood pulp papers also do.

One of the later specimens, a bank note issued during the reign of the Emperor Hung-wu, A.D. 1368-1399, is made of a darkened pulp, probably due to admixture with a little lamp black, and on it are lighter impressions from large stamps bearing the square seal letters. It is just possible that these marks may be of the nature of watermarks, and were impressed while the pulp was soft and wet, but it is not possible now to take the bank note up from the cardboard on which it has been pasted, as to do so would probably cause it to fall to pieces, so it cannot, for the moment, be properly examined.

Corean and Japanese papers were the same as Chinese, and they all look as if there are no wire marks or watermarks upon them, with the one exception I have mentioned, but Dr. Wiesner says that by the ninth century marks show in many instances which prove that papers were made in moulds or sieves with network bottoms, the impression of which remains like our "chains" or laid marks. In the King's Library at the British Museum is shown a piece of Oriental paper, an official letter in Coptic, dated A.D. 1048. It does not look so strong or good as the Chinese paper, but resembles thin blotting paper, and shows no wire mark.

An early example of European paper is preserved in the Record Office in London. It is a letter from the Count of Toulouse to Henry III., and is dated A.D. 1216. In France, however, by this time, the making of paper had been understood for some time, as it was made there in 1189. In Belgium it was not made until 1551, in which year a paper mill was set up at Tourneppe by Henri de Nevere.

Fig. 54.—Watermark used by John Tate in 1495.

By the end of the fifteenth century paper-making in Europe was perfectly understood, and the papers of that date, and for some time after it, are frequently excellent in every way, and as sound, strong, and good now as they were when first made.

The first English book printed on English paper is Bartholomaeus, *De Proprietatibus Rerum*, published 1495-6. The paper is of high quality, it shows a fine wire mark, and a watermark of a double circle enclosing an eight-pointed star. The paper was made at Hertford by John Tate, who was afterwards Lord Mayor of London; the title page is cut in wood, and the book is illustrated with outline wood-cuts.

At the end are some verses, and among these occur the lines:—

"And John Tate the younger Joye mote he broke,
Which late hath in England doo make this paper thynne,
That now in our Englysch this boke is prynted Inne."

It is paper to be proud of, and John Tate the younger would unquestionably look upon the large majority of our modern papers with the utmost scorn, and he would be perfectly justified in doing so.

The early method of making paper was to allow the pulp to settle at the bottom of a trough like a sieve, with a wire bottom, in which the wires were arranged in a certain way, thick and thin, the trade mark of the maker also being outlined in wire. The faint marks these wires cause in the paper are called watermarks, and although at first they were makers' marks, they eventually denoted the size of the sheet of paper on which they were shown.

The present method of making paper from rags is to pulp them thoroughly in water, and let the white particles become so thoroughly diffused that the liquid in which they float looks like thin milk.

This thin mixture, however, if left quiet, very quickly resolves itself into a sediment of white fibres with clear water above them. If now the superambient water can be drawn off, and the sediment pressed flat, paper is the result. But it is not so easily done as said. In order to catch the sediment in the most satisfactory way, the milky fluid containing the rag fibres is allowed to flow in a thin stream over a long, shallow trough, which is kept moving onwards and is also so arranged that it has a sideways tremble, backwards and forwards as well. The effect of this is that when the further end of the trough is reached, on its floor there is a thin continuous film of slightly matted fibres, the water from which has flowed away along the sides of the trough. Now another device comes into play; a thin light roller of wire presses lightly on the wet film, and by this pressure the little fibres are pressed upon each other so that they mat, interlace, and cohere together. The paper in this state is of course very delicate, but by reason of a quick drying and carrying off on light rollers it soon acquires the strength necessary to enable it to hold together until it is quite dry. Then it goes through several other stages, the most important of which is pressing. The various processes can obviously be modified easily enough so as to make a thin paper or a thick one. Paper made in this way with a vibratory trough is called "machine made," and by reason of its fibres laying more or less in a uniform direction the resulting paper is more easily torn in one direction than in the other. If a circular piece be cut out of such pulp and laid on water it will tend to fold up two of its opposite sides.

But ancient paper was made in a trough held by hands and given a lateral movement, then pressed and dried in some simple way. By such a procedure the fibres are thoroughly mixed, and do not lie in one direction more than in another, so that if a circular bit of such paper be laid in water it will turn upwards at the edge evenly all round, and look like a little saucer.

I have mentioned a light wire roller which presses the wet film more or less into shape just before it leaves the long trough to be dried. As long ago as the thirteenth century in Europe the fact that devices could be impressed upon the undried film by thinning it and making it more transparent where touched appears to have been known, and from about that time onwards "watermarks" have fortunately been applied in the same manner, namely, so as to come in the middle of the first leaf of the pair forming a folio. It is also fortunate that the "chains" or wires forming the rollers have always been laid in the same way; it is certainly the obvious one, but obvious ways are not always adopted. The result is that by observing the direction of the strong chain marks and the fine "laid" marks between them much information concerning the folding of the original sheets can be obtained.

In very early papers these rules cannot be safely followed, because early chain marks as well as early watermarks were not produced in the same reliable way. The paper being made in moulds with wire netting at the bottom, the impression came below the paper instead of above it as in the case of the roller, and also the sizes of the sheets were more likely to differ.

Watermarks are the semi-transparent devices which show on certain pages of a printed book. They are to be seen on most papers of the fourteenth to the eighteenth centuries, and there has been a good deal written about them, especially abroad. The devices were outlined in wire and set in the bottom of the trough or on the wire roller I have just described, so that the lines are impressed upon the pulp just when it is in its most sensitive condition. The pressure from the wire device thins the pulp wherever it is touched, and so when dry the device shows lighter than the rest of the paper.

These marks should be called wire marks rather than watermarks, and the French word for them, "Filigranes," is more correct than ours. The difference in tint between a watermark and the rest of the paper is so distinct that a photographic negative placed under one will render a capital photograph of it, far better than any drawing, but it needs a long exposure.

Watermarks are already of considerable value to Bibliographers, and it is likely that in the near future they will be much more noticed, especially in English books. Many frauds have already been detected by reason of the watermarks, as it is a point that *faussaires* have so far paid little attention to. The marks are, however, not to be relied on after about 1750, as they do not run reliably in machine made or wove papers.

Armorial devices have been largely used as watermarks. Many of the earlier marks show the arms of towns, especially continental ones, and among others there are the arms of France, Portugal, William and Mary and Queen Anne, shown in full heraldic outlines.

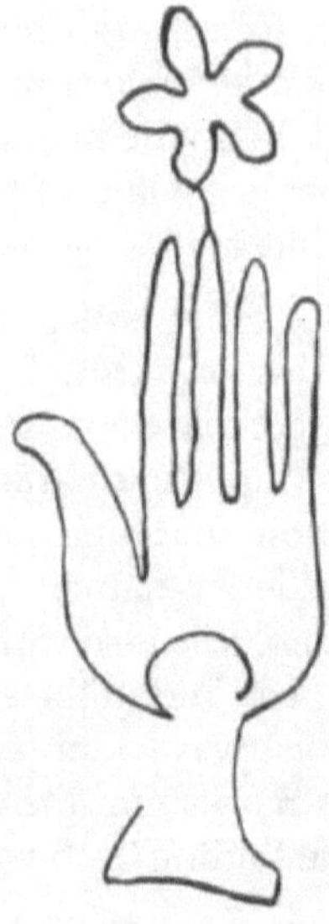

Fig. 55.—English "hand" watermark, 1512.

The Holbein family of Ravensburg bore a bull's head as their armorial badge, and they were paper makers, so the bull's head shows on their paper as a watermark. It was afterwards much copied, and during the fifteenth and sixteenth centuries it became a favourite mark on German papers. There does not seem to have been any strict copyright in any of the devices used as watermarks. They were freely used by any one who cared to do so, but the copies were never very carefully made, they were always variants of the original. They were moreover generally accompanied by another mark, that of the maker, on another part of the paper. The same privilege of using a "maker's" mark was also allowed to the silversmiths in addition to the official hall mark.

To some slight extent watermarks on paper made for particular books have followed the subjects of those books, and in accordance with a loyal feeling there are instances of a crown watermark being used on paper prepared for special copies of books intended for presentation to reigning sovereigns.

Fig. 56.—English "crown" watermark, 1745.

On papers used for early English printed books we find the favourite German bull's head, bunches of grapes, unicorns, dogs, hands with stars, and shears. These appear in several sizes, and show many varieties and modifications of their original designs.

In the sixteenth and seventeenth centuries a greater variety occur; on English paper there is found the post horn and the fool's cap, sometimes showing as a cap only and sometimes as a fool's head with cap and bells. A similar design was largely used abroad. In the time of Charles I. a crown was a usual watermark on official folio paper, but the Rump Parliament ordered that the foolscap should be in future substituted for it, which was done. "Double foolscap" is still used as a designation for a certain size of printing paper, so also is "double-crown."

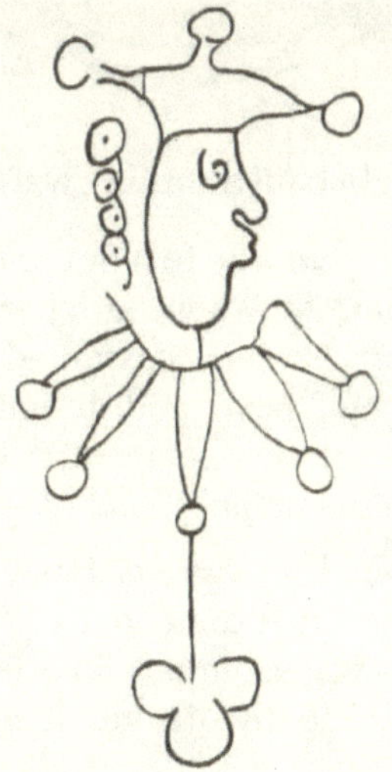

Fig. 57.—English "foolscap" watermark, 1661.

Fig. 58.—English "Britannia" watermark, 1907.

The foolscap itself shortly gave way to a figure of Britannia or a lion rampant. The post horn was another common watermark here; it gave its name to its paper about 1670, when the mail carrier was accustomed to announce his approach by a blast from his horn. The name "Post" still designates a certain size of printing paper. The smallest folio paper of the seventeenth century was marked with a watermark of a "pot," and hence the name.

For specially printed books it is a pretty fancy to have a coat-of-arms set as a watermark, and it is now and then done, but I fear few readers notice it. Many papers are now made without watermarks, and it is likely enough that, except for trade terminology, they will gradually die out altogether as being unnecessary.

The possibilities of artistic watermarking have not yet been fully realised. At the St. Louis Exhibition in 1904 there was a German exhibit which showed the remarkable effect which could be made by impressing paper pulp by means of a photographic plate in relief.

Fig. 59.—English "post" watermark, 1679.

Fig. 60.—English "pot" watermark, 1640.

The papers which had been so treated were set up in a frame with a light behind them, and they looked like most delicate paintings in monotone. Those exhibited were portraits of celebrities, and they were not only excellent but possessed the quality of permanence in a remarkable degree.

Printing papers are generally white, but sometimes they have been used in colour, green, pink, blue or yellow. Such papers are now and then found in Italian, German, and English books, more rarely in French. Silk and satin have both been used for printing on in England from the seventeenth to the nineteenth century. Vellum has also been largely used for special copies of fine printed books.

A recent French book of prayers is entirely woven in white and black silk. It looks like a beautifully printed book with monotone borders.

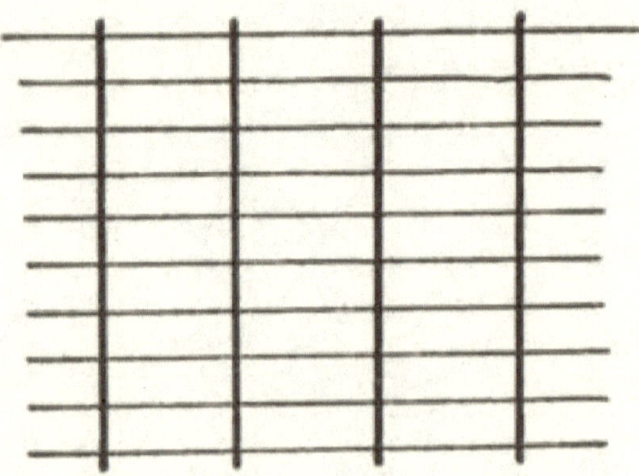

Fig. 61.—"Chain lines" thick, and "laid lines" thin, on paper.

An original sheet of paper can of course be made and cut to any size, and the terms folio, quarto, octavo, and duodecimo do not indicate any actual size except in bookbinders' specifications. The terms only indicate the number of times the original sheet has been folded, and this obviously is a matter which is subject to as much variation as the printers choose. But fortunately such foldings do not vary much, and so we may safely mention those that are most commonly used. There are several ways of finding this out, the most obvious being to count the leaves which follow any one letter in the white line at the bottom of the leaf. This letter is called the "signature." If there is an A or A 1 at the bottom of the first leaf, and when eight leaves have been turned over a B or B 1 appears, then the book is an octavo, and so on. Another way of determining the same thing is by means of the direction taken by the chain or wire marks all over the paper, and yet another is to be found by studying the position of the watermark. But neither of these tests are conclusive, and often enough there are neither chain marks nor watermarks to be found at all, and the sheets are not always rightly or carefully cut, which brings the watermark all wrong, so the following notes are only what may be expected in normal books.

If a piece of paper or page of a book printed before 1750, and possibly in later work, be held up to the light, certain lines may be seen all over it in a lighter tint than the rest of the page. These appear as long thick lines crossed at right angles by short thin ones. The long thicker lines are known as "chain" lines, and the shorter ones "laid" lines, and they are of some value when they exist for helping to determine the "size" of the book.

Fig. 62.—Fol.

—Fol. If the original sheet is folded once it is called a folio, and in this case the chain marks are perpendicular and the watermark is in the middle of the first leaf. In a folio there is one fold, two leaves or four pages, and nothing to cut. Most of Caxton's books are folios although they are quite small.

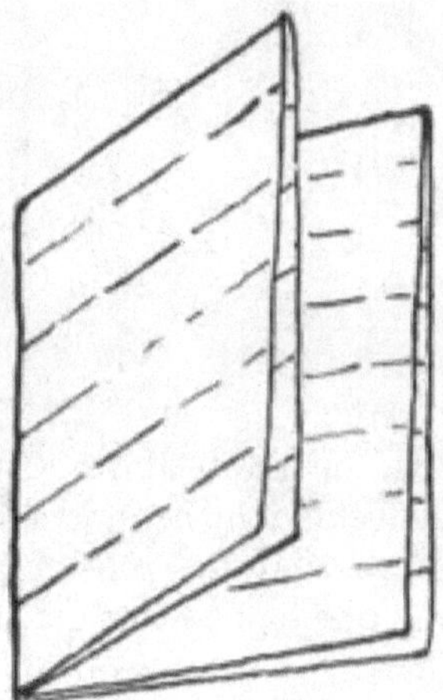

Fig. 63.—4°.

—4° in size. If the once folded sheet be folded again across the other way we get a gathering with four leaves, or eight pages, called a quarto. The chain lines are horizontal, and the watermark in the middle of the back of pp. 4 and 5; there are two foldings and two tops of leaves to be cut.

—8°. If the quarto be again folded we get a gathering of eight leaves, or 16 pp., called an octavo, which is the commonest size for English books. In an octavo there are three foldings, the chain lines are perpendicular, the watermark is quartered at the tops of pp. 3, 4, 11 and 12, and there are two tops and two fronts to be cut.

The further foldings of 16°, 32°, and 64° are the same operations carried further, but although such sizes do exist they are so uncommon that a further description of them is not necessary.

—12°. In the case of a duodecimo a different initial folding is followed. The original sheet instead of being folded once across the middle, as in the case of a folio, is now folded into three equal divisions. The parallelogram thus formed is folded across its shorter diameter, and this again along its longer diameter. There is now a gathering of twelve leaves, or 24 pp., with four foldings, the chain marks perpendicular, the watermark halved at the tops of pp. 3 and 9, and there are two tops and four fronts to be cut. It is the commonest size of the smaller French books.

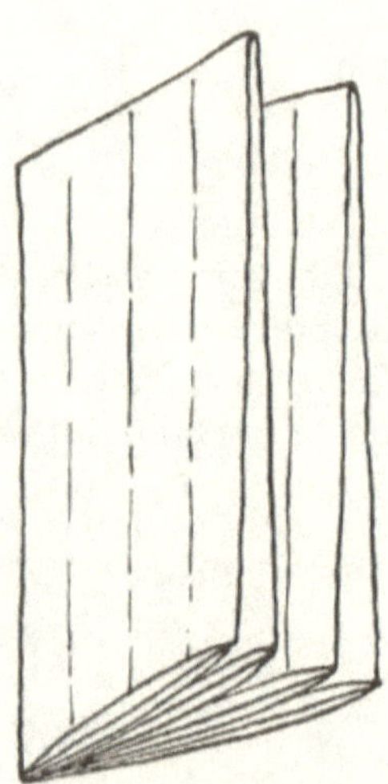

Fig. 64.—8°.Fig. 65.—12°.

As to sizes, folios run from the great Atlas of Charles II., measuring five feet nine inches and a half by three feet two inches and a half, and requiring eight skins of morocco for its binding, to the tiny *Galileo a Madame Cristina de Lorena*, 1615, "imprimé en 1897," measuring one half by one quarter of an inch. A folio cannot be recognised by its shape.

The sizes of quartos and octavos are also very varied, but, roughly speaking, they can be recognised by their shapes, especially in the case of modern books. A quarto is generally squarish in outline, nearly as broad as it is long; an octavo is an elongated rectangle, its breadth considerably less than its length. A duodecimo is always much longer than its breadth.

As curiosities, books have been made in many forms, circular, heart-shaped, octagonal, flower or animal forms, but they are of small importance, and have been chiefly made as Christmas cards, valentines, and such ephemeral publications.

The rules as to quiring of books printed on paper do not apply to books printed on vellum. Such books are always folios, and they are generally quired in gatherings of ten leaves, following the fashion used in the ancient manuscripts, but, of course, they can equally well be gathered together in any even number that may be preferred. There is no rule.

In Europe, until the nineteenth century, paper was always made from triturated rags, but the demand for cheap literature which has become so urgent in recent years has compelled paper manufacturers to find some commoner material from which to make their paper.

It is possible that the way out of the difficulty was suggested by an analysis of Japanese paper. This has been known here for some time. It is strong, soft, and valuable for many reasons, and is cheaply made of fibres from plants of the mulberry tree species. Japanese paper is hand made and has a certain amount of dressing, its surface is dull, but takes impressions from engraved plates or type easily. It appears to last fairly well, but would probably not stand much wear at the joints.

The idea of using pulped vegetable matter for paper was, however, not new, even to the Japanese, as there was such a thing as paper made from papyrus, but it does not seem to have been much employed, because it was not necessary in view of the fact that the papyrus did quite well by itself without any further manipulation.

For reliable papers, the Committee on the Deterioration of Paper appointed by the Society of Arts in 1898 give in their report a statement that 70 per cent. should consist of fibres of cotton, flax, or hemp, but about the middle of the nineteenth century it was found that passable paper could be very cheaply made from straw and from esparto grass, and this paved the way for the disastrous use of mechanical wood pulp for cheap newspapers and books.

Many sorts of wood pulps are now made for this purpose, and there is no doubt that the industry of breaking up wood for the purpose of paper making is a large and increasing one. In Norway there are several large establishments already working at this output. The fibres of spruce, pine, birch, poplar, jute, and manilla are all extensively used. The wood is cut up into small pieces and triturated until it is in a state of fine dissemination, a mass of small fibres, in which condition it is mixed in certain proportions with the other materials of which the paper is to be composed. In spite of the warnings of the Society of Arts Committee, there is no doubt that the use of "mechanical" wood pulp for paper is increasing, and this regardless of the fact that there is no lasting quality in such material, for the fibres of the wood are invariably brittle, and they also darken rapidly under the influence of light.

The dressing of such papers with resin or gelatine effects a certain improvement; gelatine particularly adds to the life of a paper and increases the elasticity of the wood fibres, but this good effect tends to die out in time. Resin is of less use.

One particularly troublesome result of having to deal with wood pulp papers is that it will not hold the threads used in ordinary binding; the thread cuts right through the paper because of the shortness or brittleness of the fibres, and if a book printed on such paper has to be bound, the only safe way to do it is to frame each page in a border of sound rag paper, and then have it sewn as usual. Wood paper will not stand bending, but breaks off short if there is anything like a joint or fold in it, and the framing or mounting prevents this. The process of mounting every leaf of a book is, however, a very expensive one; a couple of pounds may well be spent on a comparatively small book for this operation alone, so that the prospect before owners of libraries who wish to keep their books in good order is not brilliant. No amount of dressing can make such paper really strong, as it is the fibres themselves that are in fault.

But there is another form in which the use of wood is not so harmful, and in this case the fibres are no longer there to be found fault with. "Chemical" wood pulp is a form of cellulose, and it is likely that it is destined to play an important part in the paper of the future, in conjunction with fibres of various sorts.

Chemical wood pulp is prepared from the wood fibres by "digesting" with caustic soda or bisulphide of lime, as reducing agents. The process is one of much interest, and moreover a good deal of wood has to be used to make a comparatively small amount of wood cellulose. Esparto and straw celluloses are not so good as wood cellulose.

The invention of the "half-tone" process, by which a dotted block can be produced from a toned drawing, print, or photograph, can be made, is responsible for much dangerous procedure with regard to the paper upon which the prints from the dotted blocks are to be made.

In itself the invention of the half-tone process is a wonderful and beautiful one, but it has done more to ruin the already decadent modern paper than anything else, because it has made the dressing of the paper of greater importance than the paper itself.

Incidentally, the half-tone block has given the death-blow to the old and beautiful art of wood engraving, which is now only found in quite exceptional instances. But the half-tone block has, nevertheless, provided some small solace for the dispossessed wood engravers, because the soft metal blocks go wrong in light places and themselves need careful revision with a graver. This touching-up is so general, and so much technical skill is required for its proper execution, that it has already become a recognised profession, and the engraver's name is often enough recognised in the lettering of the prints made from such blocks, especially in American publications.

The dots of half-tone blocks were at first of an easily visible size, but as the method of production became better understood it was found that they could be made so small that they were no longer visible as separate dots to the unaided vision, but that the effect produced was really that of a tone-wash.

But the very finely grained blocks were difficult to print from, the ink stuck too readily between the dots, where it was not wanted, and the surface of the paper was not even enough to give a clear impression, even if it was calendered and super-calendered. So something had to be done to give the paper a more level surface, and the needed material was found in china clay mixed more or less with barytes. It is laid down in the *Society of Arts Report* that the amount of this dressing should in no case exceed 10 per cent. in any paper, but modern "art" papers have for a long time much exceeded this fair proportion.

From the beginning some kind of dressing has always been found necessary in the manufacture of paper, but nothing so dangerous as china clay has ever been used. The net result is that almost all modern editions-de-luxe, and fine illustrated books generally, either having half-tone plates or colour plates done by the three colour process, consist of little else but thin sheets of china clay supported by the smallest possible skeleton of wood or other cheap fibres.

It must be at once granted that the impressions from delicate half-tone blocks made on clay paper are admirable, and it is also true that the printing ink makes the clay insoluble in water wherever it touches it. But the clay has a certain affinity for damp, and books printed on clay paper very readily show damp stains, and if left for any time in a really damp place they are liable to become solid bricks of white mud, quite impossible to repair.

If very dry the non-cohesive clay will turn to a white powder. Moreover, this clay-laden paper will not hold binding threads, so again it has to be preserved. A book printed on such material has to be treated in the same way as I have described in the case of wood pulp paper.

There is, however, a plan of preserving prints on clay, and this is to fasten down the printed portion on a piece of sound paper from the beginning. This is already done to some extent, and it should be universal in the case of isolated plates, but when a book is all printed on clay paper, as many fine and valuable books unfortunately are, it is difficult to say what is best to be done. The only real remedy seems to be a refusal on the part of purchasers to buy such books. But purchasers do not always know when they are buying clay instead of paper. It is, however, not difficult to tell, as the clay-laden paper feels very smooth and soft to the touch of a dry finger. This peculiarity can be easily detected in one or other of the American magazines, Harper's or Scribner's, and the difference between the feel of a page holding an impression from a fine half-tone block, and that having only text, will at once be evident.

If a mark may be made on a suspected sheet, a drop of water should be put upon one corner, left a second or two, and then dried off with blotting-paper. Now a light scrape with a knife over the damped place will remove a layer of white clay if it is there.

There is no doubt that the large majority of our modern books will not be in readable condition in about a hundred years' time from the date of their publishing.

BOOKS TO CONSULT.

Paper.

Arts, Society of. — Report on the Deterioration of Paper. *London*, 1898.

Blades, W. — (*Athenæum*, March 30th, 1889, p. 409. Paper on Watermarks).

BLANCHET, A.—Essai sur l'histoire des Papier. *Paris*, 1890.

BREITKOPF.—Versuch die Einfuhrung des Leinenpapieres. *Leipzig*, 1784-1801.

BRIQUET, C. M.—La Legende Paléographique du Papier de Coton. *Genève*, 1884.

BRIQUET, C. M.—Recherches sur les Papiers du xe au XIVe siècles. *Paris*, 1886.

CAMPREDON, E.—Le Papier. *Paris*, 1901.

CHARPENTIER, P.—Le Papier. 1890. (Frémy, E.)

DUNBAR, J.—Notes on the Manufacture of Wood Pulp Papers. *Leith*, 1892.

ERFURT, J.—The Dyeing of Paper Pulp. *London*, 1901.

EVANS, L.—Ancient Paper Making. *London*, 1896.

GIRARD, A.—Le Papier. *Lille*, 1892.

GOODCHILD, G. F., and TWENEY, C. F.—A Technological and Scientific Dictionary. *London*.

GRIFFIN, R. B., and LITTLE, A. D.—The Chemistry of Paper Making. *New York*, 1894.

HERRING, R.—Paper and Paper Making. *London*, 1855.

HOERNLE, A. F. R.—Who was the inventor of Rag Paper? (*Royal Asiatic Society Journal*, October, 1903).

HOYER, E.—Die fabrikation des Papiers, 1886. (Bolley, P. A.)

KARABACEK, J.—Mittheilungen aus der Sammlung der Papyrus Erz. Rainer. Bd. II., III., 1887.

KAY, J.—Paper. *London*, 1893.

KLEMM, P.—Handbuch der Papierkunde. *Leipzig*, 1904.

LLOYD, E.—Account of a sort of Paper made of Linum Asbestinum found in Wales. (Phil. Trans., Abr. III., p. 105, 1684).

MIERZINSKI, S.—Handbuch der Praktischen Papier Fabrikation. *Wien*, 1886.

PAYEN, A.—La fabrication du Papier. *Paris*, 1873.

PIOT, G. J. C., and PINCHART, A.—Specimens des Papiers recueillis dans les diverses coll. de documents qui composent les archives générales du Royaume de Belgique. *Bruxelles*, 1872.

SARTORI, L.—L'Industria della Carta. *Milano*, 1897.

SCHAEFER, J. C.—Attempts towards making Paper from Plants and Wood. (German.) *Regensburg*, 1765.

STONHILL, W. J.—Paper Pulp from Wood and other fibres. 1885. (Rattray, J.)

VALENTA, E.—Das Papier. *Halle*, 1904.

WATT, A.—The Art of Paper Making. *London*, 1890.

WIESNER, J.—Mikroskopische untersuchung alter ostturkestanischer und anderer asiatischer Papiere. *Wien*, 1902.

WATERMARKS.

BRIQUET, C. M.—De la valeur des Filigranes du Papier comme Moyen de determiner l'age de documents. *Genève*, 1892.

BRIQUET, C. M.—Papiers et Filigranes des archives de Gêves 1154 à 1700. *Genève*, 1888.

BRIQUET, C. M.—Les Filigranes. Dict. Hist. des Marques du Papier. 4 vols. *Paris*, 1907.

CASTAN, A.—Catalogue des Incunables. *Besançon*, 1893.

DEL MARMOL, F.—Dictionnaire des Filigranes. *Paris*, 1900.

DENNE, S.—Observations on Paper Marks, 1796. (*Archæologia*, XII., p. 114).

HEITZ, P.—Les Filigranes avec la crosse de Bâle. *Strasbourg*, 1904.

HEITZ, P.—Les Filigranes des Papiers contenus dans les archives de la ville de Strasbourg. *Strasbourg*, 1902-04.

HEITZ, P.—Les Filigranes des Papiers de la Bibliothèque de Strasbourg. *Strasbourg*, 1903.

LEMON, R.—Collection of Water Marks. 1891.

MIDOUX, E., and MATTON, A.—Etudes sur les Filigranes des Papiers employés en France au XIVe et XVe siécles. *Paris*, 1868.

PIOT, G. J. C., and PINCHART, A.—Specimens des Papiers recueillis dans les diverses coll. des documents qui composent les archives générales du Royaume de Belgique. *Bruxelles*, 1872.

SERMA SANTANDER, C. A. de.—Supplément au Catalogue des livres de la Bibliothèque de M. C. de Serma Santander. *Bruxelles*, 1803.

SOTHEBY, S. L.—Principia Typographica (with examples of foreign watermarks). *London*, 1858.

SOTHEBY, S. L.—Typography of the fifteenth century (with examples of watermarks). *London*, 1845.

CHAPTER IV.

PRINTING.

Assyrian bricks, with printed inscriptions—Oiron ware—Chinese types—Block books—Costeriana—Types and stereotypes—Printing presses.

There are numbers of instances of impressions from small devices, cyphers and letterings cut on blocks of wood or soft metal and made on pieces of pottery. These stamps are the forerunners of the types with which our modern books are printed. Among these impressions those which are made on the tablets or cylinders of baked clay, many of which have been found among the ruins of Babylon and Nineveh, are by far the earliest. They are covered with inscriptions printed in cuneiform characters, and contain records of sales of slaves, loans of money, sales of land and the like, and on the larger bricks and cylinders are longer inscriptions of greater interest, among them stories of the Flood. Many of these records are contained within an outer shell of the same shape, in which is either a short title with seal or even a duplicate inscription. These outer cases are the earliest examples of anything in the shape of a cover or binding over written or printed matter. Some of the cuneiform bricks are said to date from the third thousand years B.C., and many of the later examples belonged to the libraries of Sennacherib and Ashurhani-Pal, Kings of Assyria.

Fig. 66.—Assyrian tablet of clay, impressed with cuneiform inscription. With outer case.

Similar bricks, impressed with inscriptions, have been found in North America. The letters on these bricks, tablets, or cylinders were printed letter by letter by hand upon the clay when it was wet and soft, without ink, then the brick was dried either in an oven or in the sun, so that this earliest method of printing is diametrically opposite to the modern process, in which case the letters are inked and kept rigid, while the paper or other substance on which the impression is to come is lightly pressed upon them.

In the eleventh century the Chinese made types of clay or porcelain, and set them up in a frame and printed from them, and afterwards they cut the original types in wood and made impressions, or stereotypes from them in porcelain, and when this had been baked they cast leaden types from it. Chinese and Japanese letters are always most decorative, whether in the cursive or square seal characters.

Babylonian and Assyrian tablets, cylinders, and cones of baked clay impressed with cuneiform inscriptions have proved themselves to be the most permanent and reliable form of record that has yet been invented by mankind. The hammer alone seems to be able to destroy them.

The most precious faience in the world is that variously known as "Oiron," "Henri Deux," "Diane de Poictiers," or "Faience de Saint Porchaire." There are fewer than seventy pieces of this ware known, and each example is a masterpiece, no two being alike.

It is said to consist mainly of clay found at Saint Porchaire, a village in Poiton, and not far from Oiron, and at one of these places it was probably made.

Fig. 67.—Italian book stamps impressed upon the faience de St. Porchaire.

The pieces are often ornamented with armorials and devices of Francis I., Henri II., and Diane de Poictiers, as well as those of members of the French nobility of about the middle of the sixteenth century.

There are jugs, covered cups, biberons, dishes, salts, flower vases, and candlesticks, all curiously put together in sections, and ornamented with impressions from binders' stamps run in with differently coloured clays.

This use of binders' stamps is unique, and has been made with the utmost skill and taste. Sometimes casts have been made from the stamps so that the impression shows in reversed colours. The ornamentation is like a book-finisher's work, and several of the same stamps and rolls show on contemporary Italian bookbindings. At that time there was a strong Italian influence both in French as well as in English decorative bookbindings.

It has already been supposed that the ware may have been sent as a present to Henri II. from the family of Catherine de Medici, and M. H. Delange even goes so far as to credit Girolamo della Robbia with the work. He, as well as many other Florentine craftsmen, worked in France for Francis I.

It is not now likely that any definite knowledge as to the maker of the Saint Porchaire Faience will ever be obtained, but it will always be a notable example of the high decorative importance of binders' stamps, which are designed upon certain principles, especially with regard to their combination in groups or lines of groups.

Attempts to imitate this ware have often been made, but so far they have failed; the original seems to possess qualities and peculiarities that are impossible to imitate closely. Art forgeries are now so common and so excellent that there are really very few things that cannot be copied so exactly that it is difficult to distinguish between the original and the copy, but the Saint Porchaire ware is so far one of the very few things that completely baffle the cleverest artist, and this is largely due to the curious use of the binders' stamps.

Engraved wooden blocks were used in China, Corea, and Japan as early as the sixth century, and quite likely long before. These blocks were cut in the same manner as the European block books, except that type and illustrations were not shown on the same block. In Thibet similar blocks were cut and charms were printed from them.

The use of separately engraved types which could be arranged as desired seems to have been known in these countries at about the same time, but it was not so suitable to their then requirements, and so it made no headway. They soon reverted to the simple block engraving as better. No doubt the reason of this was that the number of separate letters that might be required was so great that it was practically prohibitive. The letters both in China and Japan are still mainly in the syllabic stage, and so there are a great number of them. The alphabetical stage is, however, gradually being reached, especially in Japan.

It is very likely that the European idea of cutting block books was borrowed from China, and here from the later half of the fifteenth century until the earlier half of the sixteenth century such books were produced plentifully in Germany, Holland, and England, and more rarely in France.

Single-sheet pictures were made at first, the earliest dated example known being the "St. Christopher" of 1423, now in the Rylands Library in Manchester. From being cut on wood these curious prints are generally known as xylographs. Criticism and comparison of them is a very difficult matter, as they were designed and cut on such broad and easy lines that they were easily copied almost exactly, but now all the important and very early specimens are so well known and have been so carefully listed and described by competent bibliographers like Mr. Gordon Duff, Sir Martin Conway, Hain, Ottley, Bradshaw, Hessels, Proctor, and others, that there is little risk of fraudulent imitation remaining long unrecognised.

The block book proper however, shows text as well as illustrations, the text gradually becoming more and more important. Block books are printed in pale coloured ink, so that they may take colour as well as possible, and are usually coloured more or less, sometimes by hand and sometimes by means of stencil plates, or perhaps a combination of both methods. Many of them are astronomical, but as a rule the subjects are more or less religious, such as the "Ars Moriendi" or "Biblia Pauperum"; the illustrations and the text being variously arranged. Each page is cut on one block, sometimes printed page by page, sometimes two pages at a time, and always on one side of the paper only.

Now and then, as in the case of the "Speculum Humanae Salvationis," the text is separately cut; this remarkable book is supposed to have been printed at Utrecht about 1470-72. Block books are always printed on paper of excellent quality.

Printing from moveable types in Europe is considered by many authorities to have been invented by Laurens Janszoon Coster, of Haarlem, during the earlier half of the fifteenth century. Actual proofs are wanting, but there exist several books and fragments of books, many of which have been recovered from the boards of old bindings, which certainly are not the work of Gutenberg. These fragments were printed in Holland, and are known as "Costeriana"; several of the letters used correspond to the Dutch manuscript letters of the time, and many of them are copies of the school books known as "Donatus'." Some of the letters look much as if they had been cut in wood. At Avignon it is recorded that in 1444 experiments with printing types were made.

The Coster legend appears to have been started by Adrianus Junius, who in his *Batavia*, published at Antwerp in 1588, speaking of Haarlem, says: "Redeo ad urbem nostram cui primam inventae ist hic artis typographical gloriam deberi."

There is no doubt that the Costeriana have a family likeness between them, and the types used in them have been carefully compared by Mr. Hessels with those found in the edition of Ælius Donatus' grammars, and in the *Doctrinale* of Alex. de Villa Dei, and in his opinion they have the same origin.

Whether the rival claims of Avignon, Haarlem, or Mainz, for the honour of having been the first town in which printing from moveable types was done in Europe will ever be finally settled, is questionable. But there is no doubt that Johann Gutenberg was the first printer in Europe who made printing with moveable type of real usefulness. In 1472, Fichet wrote that Gutenberg, who worked in Mayence, was the first inventor of the art of printing by means of moveable types. Curiously enough the work credited to him shows no amateur feeling whatever. Both the Indulgences of 1454, which may be his, and the Mazarin Bible of about 1455, which certainly is, are as finely and perfectly printed as any books ever have been since.

It must be noted here that certain authorities still maintain that this Bible was printed by Fust and Schöffer, but the weight of expert opinion is nevertheless strongly in favour of Gutenberg.

But however this may be, in the case of the beautiful Mainz Psalter, we are on absolutely safe ground. In this book appears the date 1457, and also the names of the printers Johann Fust and Peter Schöffer. It is in every way a magnificent specimen of typography, and the letters are very large. It is also a fine example of colour printing, as the initial letters are cut in wood and printed in red and blue. Peter Schöffer was originally an illuminator of manuscripts, and no doubt we owe the splendid initials of the Mainz Psalter to his liking for colour.

The first printed date in a Dutch book is 1473, when books were printed both at Utrecht and Alost.

The moment separate letters were cut in wood for the purpose of printing, it must have been obvious to any workman interested in the matter that it would be far better to use them as models only, and that for actual use casts in soft metal would be more economical. In J. E. Hodgkin's *"Rariora"* there is an excellent detailed account of the manner in which types are cast.

At first the method of casting type was probably much the same as it is now, except that it was done slowly by hand instead of quickly by machines. The matrix was set at the bottom of a short funnel in a little hand press. This press was held in the left hand, funnel upwards, then a little melted metal was run in from a ladle held in the right hand. The metal set almost immediately, and the little letter was jerked out, to be trimmed by hand. What the earliest metal used for types was cannot now be known for certain, but it was probably much the same as is now used, lead with tin and antimony, and perhaps a little copper—a composition which expands in cooling. By this hand process a good workman could produce two or three thousand letters in a day.

Now things are managed differently, and there are several automatic machines which not only save the handwork of a type caster, but do the work equally well and at a much greater speed.

For the casting of separate letters the Wick Rotary type casting machine is perhaps one of the most ingenious. It consists of a horizontal wheel with radiating channels in which the matrices of the various letters are set. The wheel revolves, and as the opening of each little channel reaches a certain point a jet of type metal is driven into it and forms a letter. A little more revolution and the letter is automatically ejected and caught on an endless chain. This machine is capable of producing 50,000 letters in an hour.

The monotype is, however, even a cleverer invention because it only casts the particular letter that is wanted. An operator translates the manuscript, by means of a key-board, into a series of holes on a strip of paper. This strip then moves on to the monotype machine, which not only casts the letter indicated by each hole, but puts it in its proper place, and jerks it forward until one line is complete. On the completion of a line the machine has a spasm, and the line is driven bodily upwards, leaving a space for the next line. This is probably the printing machine of the future, as it only requires the one operator, who translates the manuscript into dots.

The methods used in the Linotype and the Monoline are somewhat similar, and effected by the use of a key-board, but instead of casting each letter, like the monotype, they cast complete lines, which are more troublesome to correct if any mistake creeps in.

When the printing press was first used is not known, but the printing of the block books would no doubt have suggested some sort of board press long before types were used in Europe. A block book might be printed by hand only, but it would be a troublesome and laborious process, and the use of a flat padded board to put over the whole block and press upon it seems obvious enough, and the screw press evolved itself out of some such expedient. The familiar napkin press with a large wooden screw and cross handle is the type of the earliest printing presses of which we possess any record, the screw presently giving way before the more effective lever handles, and it should not be forgotten that excellent results can be obtained from these old presses acting with a direct downward pressure. They are, however, very slow in action, and that is not consistent with modern requirements.

Fig. 68.—Printing press of about 1600. From Stradanus.

The Dutch were the pioneers in improvements in these presses, and W. J. Blaew, of Amsterdam, a clever engraver, printer, and mechanician of the seventeenth century, made several improvements in many of the details, especially as regards the box, table, or forme, in which the type was set. But until Charles, third Earl Stanhope, invented the iron printing press with levers, in 1800, they were always made of wood, with screw handles.

Lord Stanhope was a most remarkable man. He was not only an ardent politician but also a notable man of science and an inventor. Among other things we owe to him the Stanhope lens; a system of logotypes, which was not received by the printing trade with much sympathy, because it lessened the need for hand labour, improvements in stereotyping, and above all the Stanhope press, which would have made a fortune for its inventor if he had wanted it. Lord Stanhope, however, gave his press to the Clarendon Press at Oxford, in exchange for a pension to his assistant. This press with its levers was for a long time the model for all printing presses used in this country.

But before the Stanhope press was invented, W. Nicholson, of London, had patented, in 1790, a device which was destined to supersede Lord Stanhope's lever press and all others like it. This was the use of a revolving iron cylinder driven by steam to carry the paper over the inked surface of the type. Nicholson's invention fell flat so long as it remained in his hands, but in about 1807 it was taken up by Koenig, of London, improved, and put upon the market, and it attracted the attention of Mr. Walter, of *The Times*.

In the issue of this paper on the 20th of November, 1814, readers were informed that it was printed by steam machinery driving the cylinders holding the paper. By cylinder presses upwards of 9,600 impressions can be made in an hour. Minor improvements since that time have been legion, and it may safely be said that no more wonderful sight is to be seen in the whole of London than the printing of one of our great daily papers.

Newspapers are usually printed from stereotypes fixed on cylinders; but books are always printed from *flat* formes, the paper being applied by cylinders. Paper can now be printed on both sides simultaneously. In Rotary machines both the printing as well as the receiving surfaces are arranged on cylinders.

The locking up of type in the case of long books was soon found to be a great inconvenience, and the idea of making a cast of such type in the form of a block, so as to set the original type free, was an obvious one. It was not, however, put into practical form until the early part of the nineteenth century, when someone unknown made casts from book types in plaster of Paris. Lord Stanhope made several improvements in this, and it is possible that the use of softened paper pulp—flong—for this purpose was his invention. Whether this is true or not, paper was certainly used for stereotyping in France about 1850, and it has been universally used in this important connection ever since.

The paper pulp is hammered on to the type by means of a hard brush, in exactly the same way that antiquaries make impressions from incised rock sculptures. The antiquaries, however, make their casts from the paper moulds in plaster of Paris, but the printer makes his in soft metal.

When the paper mould is properly dry and hard the melted metal is poured over it, and makes a perfect cast. Such casts can either be used flat for book printing, or curved to fix on cylinders for newspaper printing. The metal used is practically the same as type metal. It sets very quickly, and the heat necessary to melt it is so low, that several casts can be made from one paper mould.

Another way of making a harder printing plate is by means of a galvanic battery. In this case the mould from the type is made in wax, either impregnated or carefully dusted with black lead, and these moulds, when correct, are put into a galvanic bath, where a strong metallic deposit is laid all over them, the deposit being afterwards backed up with alloy.

Good types have always been difficult to design. The types used in block books, and in early printed books generally, were simply copies of the handwriting of the periods to which they belonged. Even in later and in modern times certain founts have been designed on the lines of cheirographic writing, for example, the "caractères de civilité," much liked by French printers, imitated the graceful calligraphy of the eighteenth century.

But a certain differentiation in the direction of squareness soon became apparent, as we have already noticed in the case of rock inscriptions; it was found easier to cut squarely-shaped letters than rounded or cursive forms.

So letters cut for the purpose of being printed tended gradually to differentiate themselves from their written analogues, and a new kind of designing came into existence. It was, however, always necessary to preserve as much of the original form of the letters as possible, otherwise they might fail to be recognised.

Printers have always liked to show their types, and from the catalogue printed by Schöffer about 1469 to Caslon's eighteenth century specimens, there have been numbers of them made and issued. A short study of these specimens will show, firstly, how very much they are copied one from another, and secondly, that no designer of genius seems ever to have appeared. All that can be said is that some are uglier than others. It has not been for want of trying, as Geoffrey Tory shows in his *Champfleury*, but, except as to Greek types, in which Robert Procter has, by his counsel, met with much success, there is no doubt that good types for printing are rare.

In the eighteenth century P. E. Fournier caused much improvement in French types, both by his example and his writings. He was the son of a typefounder, and began as a wood engraver, but eventually followed in his father's footsteps and became a typefounder himself. Fournier published a table of types in 1737, with suggestions for designing them, but his most important work is the *Manuel typographique*, which is an important work on the subject, and had widespread influence.

In the matter of facsimiles of early printed books, it may be well here to say a word or two of warning. Photography has revolutionised many things, it has destroyed some of the minor arts, but in book production it has had far-reaching effect, much of which is good.

It has also opened up several new industries, and now photo-lithographs, collotypes, half-tone blocks, and prints from line blocks made by the swelled gelatine or other processes, can be so wonderfully like the original, that a page of old printing made by one or other of these methods will often deceive an ordinary purchaser. There are many such facsimiles in the market, and the best advice I can give as to them is that very great attention should be given to the *paper* on which they are done, as this will often give the secret away. The texture and appearance of old paper is worthy of careful study, because nearly all the photo-mechanical processes need a paper which is radically different to the thick good rag-made papers which were used before cheap modern papers were thought of.

Type founding in England was first carried on in the sixteenth century, when John Day made some Anglo-Saxon types for Archbishop Parker.

Moxon, who wrote the "Mechanics of Printing" in 1693, issued the first English specimen sheet of types in 1669, and in 1776 William Caslon, "Letter-founder of London," issued a specimen of his printing types.

Two Lines Great Primer.

Quousque tandem
abutere Catilina, p
Quousque tandem a-
butere, Catilina, pa-

Two Lines English.

Quousque tandem abu-
tere, Catilina, patientia
nostra? quamdiu nos e-
Quousque tandem abutere
Catilina, patientia nostra?

Two Lines Pica.

Quousque tandem abutere,
Catilina, patientia nostra? qu
Quousque tandem abutere, Ca-
tilina, patientia nostra? quam-

Page from William Caslon's "Specimen of Printing Types." (London, 1766.)

John Baskerville, who lived and worked about the same period, was also a very eminent typefounder, but Baskerville's types were too thin in the up-strokes to be considered equal to Caslon's. Since that time such sheets of types have become common.

Late in the nineteenth century William Morris revived several of the old English block-letter types, and called them by the old names, "Chaucer," "Golden," "Troy."

WORKS TO CONSULT.

AMERICAN ART REVIEW, I.—1880, pp. 75-80. *Boston.*

BERLAN, F.—La invenzione della stampa a tipo mobile fuso rivendicata all'Italia. *Firenze*, 1882.

BLADES, W.—Who was the inventor of Printing? *London*, 1887.

BOUCHOT, H.—Le Livre. *Paris*, 1886.

BOUCHOT, H.—L'Œuvre de Gutenberg. *Paris*, 1888.

BREITKOPF, J. G. L.—Versuch die einfuhrung des Leinenpapieres, &c. *Leipzig*, 1784-1801.

BUCHER, B.—Die Faiencen von Oiron. *Wien*, 1879.

DEGEORGE, L.—L'Imprimerie en Europe aux XVᵉ et XVIᵉ siécles. *Paris*, 1892.

DELANGE, H. & C.—Recueil de ... la Faience dite de Henri II. *Paris*, 1861.

DELON, C.—Gutenberg et l'invention de l'Imprimerie. *Paris*, 1881.

DUPONT, P.—Histoire de l'Imprimerie. *Paris*, 1883.

ENCYCLOPÆDIA BRITANNICA.—Typography and Printing. By JOHN SOUTHWARD.

ENTSCHEDE, C.—L. J. Coster de uitvinder van de boekdrukkunst. *Haarlem*, 1904.

FAULMANN, C.—Illustrirte geschichte der Buchdruckerkunst. *Wien*, 1881.

FILLON, B.—Les Faïences d'Oiron. *Paris*, 1862.

FOURNIER, P. S.—Manuel typographique. *Paris*, 1764-66.

GOEBEL, T.—Fr. Koenig und die Erfindung der Schnellpresse. *Stutt.*, 1883.

HESSELS, J. H.—Gutenberg. *London*, 1882.

HESSELS, J. H.—Haarlem the birthplace of Printing. *London*, 1887.

HODGKIN, J. E.—Rariora. *London*, 1902.

JULIEN.—L'Imprimerie en chine au sixième siécle de notre eré. *Paris*, 1850.

JUNIUS, A.—Batavia. *Antwerp*, 1588.

LINDE, A. V. D.—Geschichte der Erfindung der Buchdruckerkunst. *Berlin*, 1886.

MAITTAIRE, M.—Annales Typographical. *Hagae*, 1719.

MALINKROT, B. A.—De ortu artis Typographical. *Col. Agripp*, 1639.

Martens, W. J.—Gutenberg und die Erfindung der Buchdruckerkunst. *Karlsruhe*, 1900.

Middleton-Wake, C. H.—The Invention of Printing. *London*, 1897.

Mouet.—Les machines et appareils Typographiques. *Paris*, 1879.

Monnoyer, C.—Recherches sur les origines de l'Imprimerie avant Gutenberg. *Le Mans*, 1888.

Noble.—Machine Printing. *London*, 1883.

Pollard, A. W.—Titlepages and Colophons.

Renault, R.—Debuts de l'Imprimerie. *Quebec*, 1905.

Schaafer, J. C.—Attempts towards making Paper from Plants and Wood. (German.) *Regensburg*, 1765.

Singer.—Researches into the History of Playing Cards.

Smith, G.—Assyrian Discoveries. *London*, 1875.

Solon, H. L.—History of old French Faïence. (Saint Porchaire.) *London*, 1903.

Tainturier, A.—Les Faïences dites de Henri II. *Paris*, 1860.

Vitu, A. C.—Histoire de la Typographie. *Paris*, 1886.

Wolfius, J. C.—Monumenta Typographica. *Hamburg*, 1740.

Wilson, F. J. F.—Typographic Printing Machines. *London*, 1883.

Wilson, F. J. F.—Stereotyping and Electrotyping. *London*, 1880.

N.B.—There are a large number of works on this subject, both general and concerning Printing in particular countries.

CHAPTER V.

ILLUSTRATIONS.

Wood engraving—Line engraving—Etching—Stipple—Mezzotint—
Aquatint—Lithography—Photography.

Writing in early manuscripts was continuous, no stops, no spaces, no initials.
The inconvenience of such an arrangement soon became apparent; the effect of it
can be well seen in the case of the *Codex Alexandrinus*, written in the fifth century,
although this has large initials, and the difficulty of knowing when a word ends is
bad enough, to say nothing of sentences. The manuscript is at the British Museum.

Presently the first letters of sentences, or perhaps of important words, were en-
larged or rubricated—marked in red—and from that starting point came the grad-
ual development of beautiful ornamental letters with sprays starting from them.
These sprays ultimately became rich borderings and spread all over the page, and
at last we get to the illuminated manuscripts of mediæval times filled with exquisite miniatures, borders, and arabesques of all imaginable kinds.

The subject of illuminated manuscripts has been fully dealt with by several
competent authorities, and it is not necessary here to enter into it, but so far as
printed books are concerned it will be of interest to survey shortly the chief styles
of illustrations with which they have been provided.

When printed books first began there were no illustrations in them, but initial
letters were often added in red, by hand, and other important printed letters were
marked by a dab of red or yellow across them. The outline wood cuts which shortly made their appearance were frequently intended to serve as guides for hand
colouring, and many of them are so treated.

Wood cutting in the case of block books was well understood in the fifteenth
century, but when similar illustrations appear, in company with the text, in early
printed books, the art level both of the designer and wood cutter is singularly low.
This criticism only applies to the pictorial illustrations, as in the matter of scroll
work or ornamental initials the work is excellent.

The great letter "B" in Fust and Schöffer's *Mainz Psalter*, issued in 1457, is as
fine as anything of its kind that has ever been done. It is printed from two wood
blocks which fit into each other, and which were inked alternately either red or
blue, and then printed together with the text. A slow process but thoroughly effective. The initial letters throughout this book seem to have been touched up in
places by hand, especially in the long scrolls which meander up and down the

margins of the pages.

The earliest known book illustration cut on wood is a beautiful outline sketch of the Goddess of Mercy. It is full page and illustrates a chapter from a Chinese version of the Saddharmapundarika Sutra, and was printed in 1331, nearly a hundred years before the earliest European print from a wood block, the St. Christopher, of 1423, which moreover was not a book illustration.

Chinese, Japanese, and Korean wood cuts are always in outline, thickened here and there, but quite different in character and far better in drawing and execution than early European work of the same sort. Most of the blocks from which these prints are made are of soft wood, not box, and are cut with a short knife of peculiar form set in a handle.

The drawings are made on thin paper and stuck downwards on the blocks; then the knife is carefully run along the edges of the various lines, cutting outwards, the interlinear spaces being cut away with a gouge and hammer. The wood cutting was often done by women. The method of work is probably the same as was used in Europe in the case of early blocks.

Besides the design block, always printed in dark neutral tint or black, during the eighteenth and succeeding centuries, the Chinese and Japanese cut accessory blocks which were inked in various colours. The registering of the various colour blocks was managed either by pegs or notches, and the colours were mixed with water or rice paste. Most of the European colour processes of printing require oil colours, but water colours on the Japanese principle have been used with admirable effect in some of the illustrations to Henry Shaw's books on Mediæval Dresses and Decorative Arts, and notably by Edmund Evans and his successors in more recent times.

From the earliest illustration, mentioned above, until the present day, the style of Chinese and Japanese wood illustrations has not altered. There have been several engravers of great skill in both countries, but I think the Japanese colour prints are best known to us.

The blocks are frequently signed with the names of the designers, particularly in later times, and many names are already well known to collectors.

In the seventeenth century Korin was one of the best of the Japanese illustrators; in the eighteenth century there is admirable work signed by Hokusai and Hiroshige, and among the many skilled designers of the nineteenth century the work of Kitigawa Utamaro is perhaps the best known.

The first Italian book in which wood engravings were used is, as far as is now known, the "Meditations" of Turrecremata, printed at Rome in 1467, by Ulrich Hahn. The illustrations are of a simple character in outline. Then came instances in books printed at Naples, Rome, Verona, and especially at Venice, where Erhard Ratdolt produced several with beautiful initials, borders, and pictures. Numbers of the books published at Venice in the later part of the fifteenth century are illustrated with exquisite wood cuts; among them the most celebrated and the most beautiful is the *Hypnerotomachia Poliphili*, printed in 1499.

Cum oroli deorati,gli calciamenti fopra le niuee fuffragine cú finuata
apertione,reuincti ftrictamente confibulati cú corigie traiectate per le fi-
bule doro,& altramente cú anfulette di torquei aurei cum exquifita in no
datura cómendati. Et oue era il confine dilla circunftantia dille fimbrie,
di inexcogitabile cordellatura ornate Da le moderate aure i pulfe le rotun
de & elephantine gambe fpeffe fiate alquàto manifeftare.

Elle dunque di me animaduertendo alhora,il Nympheo grado affer-
mando fteteron , uacabonde dal fuo dolce canto,repentinamente inua-
fe da quefta nouitate di me in quello loco aduenticio. Et mutuaméte ma
rauegliantife & curiofe tacitaméte explorantime,infolente gli apparue &
inufitato. In quella celebre patria homo alieno & extrario cufi a cafo effe
re puenuto . Per laquale cagione per uno poco di fpatio fteteron tra effe
una allaltra cum fecreto murmurillo,& molte fiate arimirarme fcrutarie
iclinantife.Quale fi phantafma ftato io fuffe, Ome io me fentiua in quel
puncto tutte le uifcere quaffare.Quale foglie di Accori uibráte ad gli im
petuofi uenti. Impoche apena rafficurato effendo dil crebro dicto fpaué
to,che immediate & meritaméte arbitrádo in fe hauere,oltra la códitione
hůana,altro nó conofcédo,dilla diuina uifióe dubitai che alla cinerea, Se
mele appue,Dalla fimulata forma di Beroe Epidaura decepta.Heu me da
capo icomiciai di trepidare,piu timido diuenuto,che li pauidi hymnuli
la fulua Leena di fame rugiéte uedédo.Tra me cótédétefe ad terra fuppli-

Page from the "Hypnerotomachia Poliphili." (Venice, 1499.)

This celebrated book was written by Francesco Colonna, whose name is curiously shown by the initials of the chapters, which read "Poliam Frater Franciscus Columna peramavit," "Brother Franciscus Columna loved Polia very much." Polia has been presumably identified with Lucretia Lelio, who was a native of Treviso, the place of Polifilo's dream. The many engravings are in outline, and several of them are full page.

Italians have always excelled in wood cutting, but although there have been numbers of illustrated books issued in the sixteenth and later centuries, those of the fifteenth century still remain pre-eminent. Dr. Paul Kristeller has, moreover, shown that the Italian printers devices are well worthy of attention, and many of them are very fine both in design and execution.

Block books, Japanese wood blocks, and all very early wood cuts, were cut by a knife, and such outline work, not too small, is easier to execute with a properly shaped knife than with anything else. But as soon as wood cutters began to be more skilled, and compared their work with line engraving, they found that a knife was not so useful as an engraver's burin, and so wood *engraving*, as distinct from *cutting*, came into being. The cuts in the *Nuremberg Chronicle* of 1493 show some sort of a transitional stage; there are hatchings and shadowings which would have been much more easily done with a graver than with a knife, but I believe, nevertheless, they are all knife work.

Roughly speaking, it is easier to cut a broad outline drawing with a knife than with a graver, and it is easier to cut a small detail drawing with a graver than with a knife. At the same time we must remember that a skilled engraver could execute either sort of engraving in the wrong way, just as William Harvey cut his well known wood blocks of the Death of Dentatus in such a way as to show every technical peculiarity, except one, of an engraving on metal.

Both wood blocks and metal blocks intended to illustrate printed books were always made of the same depth as the type, so that they could all be printed together, and that is done to-day in the case of process or half-tone blocks, which are actually wooden blocks faced with the soft metal bearing the design. There is always some interest in the question as to whether a certain print has been cut on a wood block or on a metal block, and if the print is in perfect condition it is a very difficult matter to decide. But it is rarely that some small defect or peculiarity does not appear by help of which a tolerably certain judgment can be arrived at. Early engraved blocks were often used again and again until they became quite old, and at last they were got at by insects who ate small holes in them. If therefore a print shows little white circular marks upon it there is no doubt that it was made from a wood block. Instances are by no means unknown in which experts have decided that a certain block had been cut on metal, and a later impression has turned up *with worm holes in it*! The grain of wood will sometimes show on an old print, or a broken edge will show a sharp fracture indicating wood, in contradistinction to a rounded one, indicating metal.

The blacks on prints from an engraved metal plate always show very even spaces, and there are usually plenty of them, often broken, however, by small white dots, the presence of which denotes the style known as Pointille, the finest examples of which can be found among the French Horæ printed for Pigouchet in the fifteenth century. The metal used was probably a sort of pewter, lead and tin, very easy to engrave upon, and strong enough to bear many printings. But in many instances these little blocks seem to have been roughly treated and have fallen about, and the result is that outer lines which show perfectly straight in early copies, show as slightly rounded lines on late ones. This is taken as a decided proof that the original block was made of soft metal, although I am by no means certain that it is impossible for a straight edge on wood to warp into a curved line.

Prints from old wood cuts in outlines were frequently added to early printed books and painted over thickly with opaque colour so as to produce a different design. The original outline has only been used as a slight guide. Instances of these curious changes can be found in numbers of the fine vellum books illustrated in colour which were printed for Antoine Vérard at Paris in the fifteenth century.

In other cases, particularly in Italy and France, ornamental printed borders and illustrations have been very carefully painted by hand just as if they belonged to ordinary illuminated manuscripts. But the art work in all these cases is not good. The true *illuminatores* were obsolescent. A few instances of attempts at colour printing either by means of blocks or stencil plates were made by Erhard Ratdolt at Venice, and a few others.

There are two distinct schools of wood engraving, and they are easily recognised from each other whenever either of them is exclusively new, but the large majority of the more recent book illustrations cut on wood show traces of both styles.

These styles are firstly that of the black line, the type of which may be found in Caxton's *Myrrour of the Worlde* printed in 1481, and secondly that of the white line, the best type of which may be found in the *History of British Birds*, illustrated with engravings by Thomas Bewick in 1797.

In judging whether an illustration in a book is printed from a block cut and printed in the manner of a wood block, the first thing to observe is whether the black lines are pressed into the paper or not. The amount of the depression of the black lines may be very slight, but it must always be looked for because although the necessary pressure for printing from type and block is slight, still there is always some of it, and before the introduction of the modern clay-laden papers, the paper used for printing upon was always softened by damp, and consequently very susceptible to pressure. If the depression of the black lines can be recognised, the print is made from a block of some sort, and printed with a slight pressure.

William Blake's curious illustrated poems are exceptions to any rule. He was very poor and unable to afford to have his writings properly published, so he wrote and drew them out himself on copper, and then etched away the ground very strongly so as to leave his lines in relief. The plates were then printed as relief blocks. As curiosities they are of great interest, and they preserve the individual touch of the artist to just about the same extent as an etching does. The process is exactly analogous to the manner in which names or designs are etched on sword blades, key rings, knife blades and the like, only Blake allowed the acid to work a little more strongly so as to get a slightly higher relief.

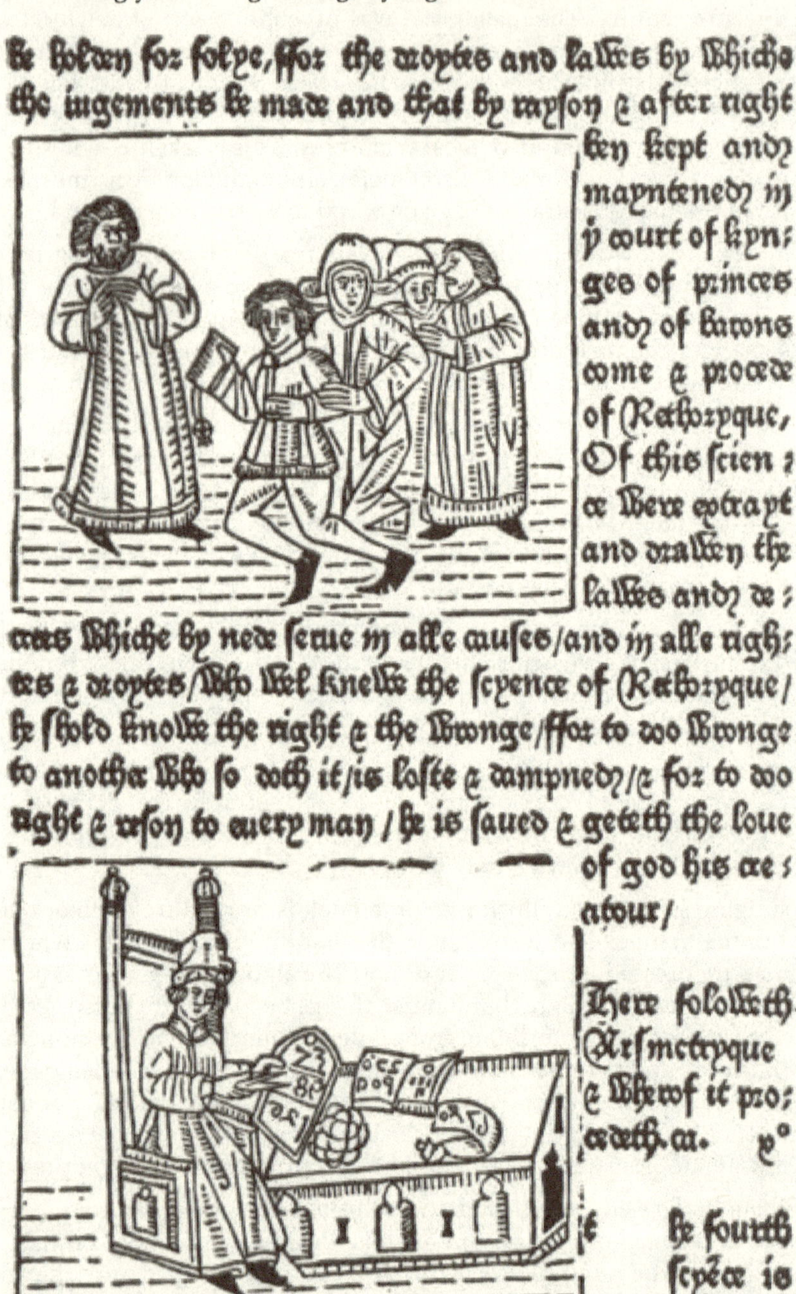

Page from Caxton's "Myrrour of the Worlde." (London, 1481.)

The first English printed book that is illustrated is Caxton's *Myrrour of the Worlde*, printed in 1481; the cuts are quite elementary in character, like all the wood cuts in English books for a long time. Ornamental borders are found in Caxton's *Fifteen Oes.*, printed about 1490.

Early English books were not freely illustrated, and it must be supposed that wood cutters were scarce. Many of the cuts used are of foreign origin. One early book is charmingly illustrated in colour; Dame Juliana Bernes' so-called *Book of St. Albans*, printed in 1486, has a long series of coats-of-arms printed from wood blocks. The colour has been added either from other blocks separately inked or else by means of stencil plates.

In the sixteenth century wood illustrations became more numerous, but many of them were still of foreign workmanship.

Borders and designs by Holbein were used by Pynson, and these had a renaissance feeling which was quite foreign to the existing style. The mixed style which consequently made its appearance is very curious. It shows well in the semi-classical device of Lucretia used by Thomas Berthelet, royal printer to Henry VIII. Towards the end of the century there were several large volumes of chronicles published in England, Halle, Grafton and Holinshed, and these and similar volumes are all well illustrated with wood cuts. Foxe's "Book of Martyrs," published in 1563 by John Day, is also an example of a well illustrated and popular book, the cuts in which were all probably made here.

Wood engravings in England gave way gradually in the seventeenth and the earlier half of the eighteenth centuries before the advancing tide of line engraving, but in the latter half of the eighteenth century Thomas Bewick came to give it a new impetus. Bewick's style was quite original, and although his particular "white line" style, good as it was, does not ever seem to have retained any hold upon the mass of engravers, yet somehow or other we find that the revival of wood cutting, both here and abroad, is generally put down to his influence.

Bewick worked on an entirely different principle to that of any of his predecessors. He gave up imitating the black line of the metal engraver and used the white line to gain his effects. No doubt this is the true theory of wood engraving. Bewick took several apprentices, many of whom afterwards became famous, but, curiously enough, none of them kept long to their master's style. In modern days Timothy Cole has revived the use of the white line; his work is most excellent and learned in every way. I have never found a wrong line in it, and if Bewick had not shown the way, and therefore put Mr. Cole in the position of a follower, the latter would have ranked as the greatest master who has ever worked on wood on the white line principle.

William Harvey was one of Bewick's apprentices; he did an immense quantity of work, which is always excellent. He soon gave up Bewick's "white line," and most of his wood engravings are like line engravings on copper. The engraving of the Death of Dentatus, after B. R. Haydon, is Harvey's most celebrated piece of work. It shows every appearance and characteristic of a line engraving, but the black marks are in intaglio. It is a *tour de force*, and cannot but be considered as a waste of energy. It was engraved upon several blocks clamped together by an iron band, and prints of it can now and then be picked up at printsellers for two or three shillings, as it is seldom recognised as a wood engraving.

"The Peacock." Wood engraving by Thos. Bewick,
from the "History of British Birds." (Newcastle, 1797-1804.)

Luke Clennell also worked with and helped Bewick, and much of his early work is like that of his master. But, like Harvey, Clennell soon evolved a style of his own. He cut some of the beautiful little cuts, after Stothard, in Rogers' "Pleasures of Memory." No doubt the Bewick training had much influence for good over Clennell's manner.

Charlton Nesbit followed Bewick closely for a time, and then, like his fellow apprentices, he worked out his own style. His work is very good and true, and he was particularly successful in his illustrations to Northcote's *Fables* and *Rinaldo and Armida*.

John Thompson was quite one of our greatest wood engravers. He worked well into the nineteenth century, and did an immense quantity of work. He engraved a celebrated set of illustrations to the *Vicar of Wakefield*, after Mulready, and was also very successful with those to Tasso's *La Gerusalemme Liberata* in 1826. His work is quite different from that of Bewick.

The nineteenth century in England was rich in numbers of excellent wood engravers, and a list of their names alone would be a long one. A proof of the high estimation in which the work of many of these artists was held is to be found in the fact that their services as engravers were freely sought by continental publishers of finely illustrated books.

J. B. Jackson, who introduced tone colour-printing, actually worked with J. M. Papillon in France in the eighteenth century. Then there were the Landells, Gray, Whimper, Wright, Folkard, and Green, and, quite late in the century, J. W. Whymper, Horace Harral, James Cooper, W. J. Linton, the Dalziels, and Swain. These two last have signed an immense quantity of excellent work, but they were large firms, and the greater part of their work was done by their workmen. Many of the artists of this time did most excellent work as designers for wood engravings, especially Sir John Millais, D. G. Rossetti, Fred. Walker, Fred. Sandys, Lord Leighton, Birket Foster, Sir E. Burne-Jones, G. du Maurier, and Cecil Lawson.

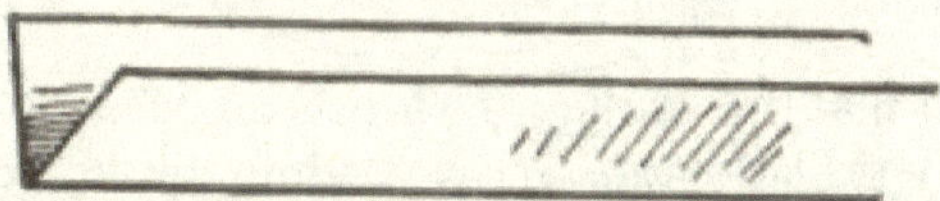

Fig. 69.—Knife for engraving on soft wood.

J. M. Papillon, who worked during the earlier half of the eighteenth century, belonged to a French family of wood engravers, and wrote a treatise about wood-cutting with the knife, which is of great interest. His work is small and excellent. Papillon makes mention of a foreigner who worked with him and used the *end* of the wood to work upon, and that he used a graver. This foreigner is supposed to have been the English artist J. B. Jackson, who was eminent here not only as an engraver, but also as the pioneer in the matter of colour-printing from wood blocks.

No doubt up to about the beginning of the eighteenth century wood cuts had been made on planed pieces of pear or other soft wood cut lengthways. The grain upon such a piece of wood necessitating the use of a knife to cut it, the knife may be a single blade or a double blade of the kind known as a "scrive," but it cannot be cut with a solid graver.

It is possible enough that to Jackson we owe the idea of making engravings on the cross-cut of a piece of wood, and if so he is entitled to great honour, as all wood work since his time has been done in that way. The graver had long been used on metal, but until the device of cutting blocks across the grain of a hard wood was thought of it could not be used on wood. Hard wood was now wanted with as little grain as possible, and box is the ideal.

In the nineteenth century much excellent wood engraving was done in France. Indeed, after a period of practical non-existence the art once more became one of great importance, and a school of wood engraving grew up that was not only very large, but the work done was of very high quality.

Bewick's style is not there, although it seems likely that the revival was really due to his influence; the old black line, resembling the engraved metal line, holds undisputed sway. Moreover, the French nineteenth century revival owes much directly to the work and influence of another great English wood engraver, J. Thompson, and with him worked an equally great French engraver, H. L. Brevière. These two men were highly gifted, and their work is always of a high order, and they met with much powerful support from contemporary engravers, followers of their own, the excellence of whose work in many instances ran their own very close.

Among the many engravers of this time whose work is always pleasant to meet with and admire we may particularly note Thiébault, S. Soyer, Sears, Porret, Roux, La Coste and both his sons, Rouget, and Nivet.

The work of many of our contemporary English engravers was also much liked in France, and they often helped to illustrate fine French books. Among the more notable of these engravers we find the names of Orrin Smith, Thomas, Samuel, and Mary Ann Williams, and A. Best.

It must be noted that the work of the artists whose work was interpreted by this school of highly-skilled engravers was admirably fitted for small book vignettes, especially the military designs so profusely issued by Meissonier, Horace Vernet, and Raffet, and, for larger work, the charming figures of Gavarni.

Augsburg in the fifteenth century was a great centre of wood engraving. A Bible with small woodcuts was issued there about 1470 by Jodoc Pflanzmann. These cuts were meant to be coloured by hand. Several other books illustrated with woodcuts were issued by Gunther Zainer and Johan Bamler.

Then notable illustrated books were published at Ulm and Lubeck, and from Nuremberg we have the great "Nuremberg Chronicle," full of woodcuts, the best of which are cut by Wilhelm Pleydenwurff and Michael Wohlgemuth. The work in this book gets away from the mere outline, and we find much clever hatching and shading, but there is much coarseness. From Basle came Seb. Brant's celebrated "Narrenschiff," one of the most popular books ever written, and illustrated with most amusing cuts of the various follies of the various sorts of fools described. Albrecht Dürer did a few illustrations for books towards the end of the fifteenth and beginning of the sixteenth centuries.

Several more illustrated wood books were issued from Nuremberg, Basle and Zurich, and some of the printers' devices were designed by Holbein.

During the seventeenth century a lull occurred in the production of German books illustrated with woodcuts; but the art has always been popular in Germany, and it never quite died out.

The very decorative "Triumph of the Emperor Maximilian," with large woodcuts, designed by Hans Burgkmeier of Augsburg in the early sixteenth century, was published in 1796. German wood engraving for books revived in the nineteenth century, and became of high excellence. German wood engravings have had a certain strength and vigour all their own from the time of the "Nuremberg Chronicle" until modern times.

Artists, moreover, have not been wanting; the quite delightful vignettes of A. Schrödter, L. Richter, G. Osterwald, R. Jordan and others, have received adequate and sympathetic treatment at the hands of engravers who are second to none. Nuzelmann, E. Kretschmar, A. Vogel, Beneworth, Joch, and the Leipzig firms of Allanson and Sears, Nicholls and Bosse, and Peupin, some of whom were foreigners.

Line engraving on a small scale plays an important part in book illustration. It is the simplest, and yet requires the most technical skill of all the methods of marking metal surfaces for the purpose of making prints. The engraver cuts out a thread of metal, producing a little track on the surface, and to do this properly requires the utmost skill.

It has been held for a long time that prints from engraved metal plates owe their existence to the proofs in sulphur which were taken from time to time from engravings intended to be filled with niello.

In the museum at Berlin there is a print on paper from an engraved metal plate, representing the Flagellation of Christ. It is German work and dated 1446. The lettering shows rightly on the print, so the engraving was made with the intent that prints should be made from it.

There is in the Bargello Museum at Florence a beautiful Pax with a nielloed plate attributed to Maso Finiguerra, the date of which is put at 1452. From this plate, before it was nielloed, prints on paper were taken, and one of them is at Paris. But the letterings on this engraving read rightly on the metal, so it was not engraved with the intent that prints should be made from it; indeed, they, as well as the impressions in sulphur, were only made to help in the working.

So that it is only safe to say that the possibility of making prints on paper from engraved metal plates was known about the middle of the fifteenth century both in Germany and in Italy.

To make a print from an engraved plate requires great pressure, as the paper has to be forced down into every mark, and the resulting mark on the paper is consequently always in relief.

The principle of a print made from an engraved wood block is that the projecting parts are covered with a thin film of ink, and when the paper is lightly pressed down upon these lines it picks up the ink from the surface wherever it touches it. In the case of an engraved metal plate, the lines on which are cut in the same way and with a similar graver to that used for white line engraving on wood, the inking and printing is quite different. Now it is the incised lines which print black, and in order to ensure this the whole plate is well rubbed over with ink so as to fill up all the incised lines, and then the unengraved polished surface is carefully wiped clean so as to leave the ink sticking in all the dots, lines and curves. Now damped paper is very strongly pressed upon the inked plate, so as to be squeezed right down into every dot, line and curve. The paper consequently is in relief wherever it has been pressed into a depression, and as there was ink there waiting for it, it will be found to have picked up and absorbed all the ink, so that the print shows black lines in low relief.

It will be easily realised that a print from an engraved metal plate cannot be printed with ordinary type at the same operation a wood-block can, so that whenever a book occurs in which such engravings show on the same page with type, there must have been two printings, one strong for the engraving and one light for the type.

We find, therefore, that in several instances where engraved illustrations have been used for a book which is for the most part printed from type, that the small piece of text which comes on the same page as the engraving, is also engraved. Not only this, but from time to time entire books have been engraved, illustrations as well as text. The finest English example of such work is to be found in the beautiful edition of the works of Horace, plentifully illustrated and engraved throughout on copper by John Pine. It was published in 1733-7.

John Sturt, who engraved numbers of book frontispieces, also produced a Book of Common Prayer, engraved throughout on silver, in 1717. He also engraved many of John Ayres' calligraphic works. Abroad, especially in France and Germany, small books have been engraved, in the seventeenth and eighteenth centuries, by P. Moreau, F. Mazot, Druet, and others, but none of them are as important as the English. Music books are engraved, and so are numbers of calligraphic books of small interest.

The first line engravings illustrating any book appear in Bettini's "Monte Santo di Deo," printed in 1477. They are said to be after designs by Botticelli. Some of the prints are full page and others are printed on the same paper as the text. They are not very good. The same kind of illustration appears in Dante's "Divina Commedia," printed in 1481. Some of these prints are, however, pasted in, but a few are on the same paper as the text.

The great excellence of Italian book illustrators on wood seems to have eclipsed all other kinds. Italian line engravers have excelled in large plates, but in books there is little of this kind of work that is at all good. Examples of small work of the kind were done in the eighteenth century by Grandi, Schedl, Pomarade, I. Frey, and C. Gregori.

In English books line engravings do not appear until 1521, when an edition of Galen published at Cambridge possesses an engraved border.

Raynald's "Byrthe of Mankind," published in 1540, has engraved plates. From this time engravings appear at intervals until towards the end of the sixteenth century, when frontispieces and portraits, always printed on separate paper and inserted as extra leaves, became common.

In the seventeenth century the same style prevailed, engraved portraits and frontispieces, but gradually small pictures came into use. The plates are often signed, and we find the name of Renold Elstrack, who worked also in the preceding century, Marshall, Hole, Cecil, Grover, and others of less merit.

In the eighteenth century native engravers seem to have given way to foreigners, and the same thing happened during the early nineteenth century. We find many beautiful engravings in English books signed by Du Bosc, Grignion, Scotin, De Launay, and others. Later, in the nineteenth century, our English line engravers rallied, and we owe much beautiful work to them. Many of their names are widely known, and their work will be more highly appreciated as time goes on, especially as this small line engraving is practically a lost art.

The Keepsake, published by Charles Heath, 1827-57, started the fashion in England of small books illustrated with delicate engravings on steel, but it must be noted that although there is engraved work in them, the greater part of the work is really etched. Exquisite work in this style was done by W. Finden, D. Allen, C. Rolls, T. C. Lewis, J. H. Robinson, E. Goodall, H. and R. Wallis, W. R. and D. Smith, W. Humphreys, John Pye, T. S. and F. C. Engleheart, F. and J. Goodyear, and these engravers were supplied with beautiful subjects by several of the eminent contemporary artists, J. M. W. Turner, Stothard, Samuel Prout, and numbers more.

Among the best examples of finely illustrated books of this period the two volumes of Rogers' *Italy* and *Poems* may safely be noted. They were published in London in 1830, and the very best results were aimed at in their production. They are uniform, and usually bound in red watered silk.

Large numbers of small books illustrated profusely with line engravings were published about the middle of the nineteenth century. They often have engraved title-pages, with little pictures in them, the full page illustration being inserted throughout. The names of both artist and engraver are usually added at the lower edge of the print.

There are *Oriental Annuals, Landscape Annuals, New Year's Gifts, Friendship's Offerings, Comic Offerings, Juvenile Forget-me-nots*, and a host of similar periodicals, and good work is to be found in all of them. They were either bound in thin panel stamped leather or else in watered silk, and in either case the binding is of interest, and wherever it exists it should be carefully preserved. A quaint little woodcut often appears in these books, printed with the text.

Besides the engravers whose names I have already mentioned, there are many others whose work appears more particularly in small periodical publications; among these may be noted J. C. Armytage, Geo. Corbould, Charles and J. Heath, James Mitan, John Sharpe, R. J. Baker, W. Greatbach, J. C. Edwards, W. Fry, W. Chevalier, S. Davenport, H. Robins, C. Warren, T. J. Williams, J. Cousins, W. Miller, S. Sangster, R. Rhodes, F. Bacon, R. J. and E. Portbury, T. Willmore, R. Brandard, J. H. Kernot, W. D. Taylor, and G. Hollis.

After about 1850 small line engravings in books began to disappear, and now they are rarely if ever done. In fact, line engraving has been killed by mezzotint and photography, and now takes refuge in its original goldsmiths' use, or in book plates.

Line engraving in France did not appeal to popular taste until a comparatively late period. The block engravings in the "Horae" of the fifteenth century, although they were line engravings, were cut in the manner of wood blocks, and the method of printing from them was different to that used in the case of ordinary metal engravings. In the seventeenth century there were several beautiful books illustrated by line engravings by Sebastian Leclerc, L. Gaultier, J. Sauné, F. Chauveau, Le Mire and H. J. Duclos.

In the eighteenth century in France the graceful designs of Ch. Eisen and J. H. Fragonard found many worthy interpreters. La Fontaine's fables and stories provided a suitable literature for these illustrations, and among them may perhaps be found the high water mark of small line engraving. Indeed, the work is all so good that any choice becomes almost invidious; but quite beautiful work was done by J. B. Patas, Choffard, N. Le Mire, De Longueil, L. Bosse, Delvaux, Johannot, Leroux, Lefebre, Ficquet, Mottet, Prevost, J. B. Tillard, J. L. Delignon, C. L. Lingée, Dupréel; and then come L. Halbon, J. Aliamet, J. Dambrun, J. B. Simonnet, P. Trière, C. S. Gaucher, and many more, some of whom worked also in the next century.

In the nineteenth century the French level of small engraved illustrations remained exceptionally high, especially in the earlier half, but many of the plates have much etching mixed up with line work; this may very likely mean that the work was done on steel, which will admit of the production of large editions; but steel is very difficult to engrave, although it is quite easy to etch. Among the line engravers who used accessory etching I have noted Pauquet, Aze, P. Choffard, and De Villiers.

The engravers whose work may be safely considered of high quality are R. De Launay, Bertonnier, Villerey, P. Savart, H. Dupont, Girardet, J. P. Marillien, L. Petit, J. F. Ribault, Chifflart, and V. Foulquier. Towards the end of the century photography came and gradually crowded out the small line engravers.

An etching is a drawing done with a needle point upon a sheet of metal protected by a thin impervious coat of soft varnish. The lines made by the etching needle pierce the varnish or "ground," and reach down to the metal, usually copper, exposing it in those places. When the drawing is complete the plate is put into a bath of strong water, usually dilute nitric acid, and wherever the surface is not protected by the ground the acid will eat away the metal.

When now the ground is cleaned off with the help of turpentine, the original design will be seen transferred to the surface of the copper in the form of dull lines, shallow if the acid has only been allowed to act for a short time, but broad, deep and irregular if the "biting" has been long. So that an etching always has a little more "effect" than was put into the original work.

It is not necessary here to enter into the mysteries of "stopping out," and several other variations of procedure, but it is sufficient to say that variations of tone and texture *can* be obtained; but, in fact, so far as book illustrations go, the etchings

I know of are always simple, and the best of them are those by George Cruick-shank.

The printing of etchings is analogous to that of line engravings, and a similar ink is used. A strong press is required, the paper is damped, and the impression is in slight relief. Line engravings are always printed in the same way as a visiting card, the untouched parts are clean, and print white, but in the case of etchings more ink is usually left, so that the untouched surfaces often show grey, none of the ink having been allowed to remain upon the plate. The French call this "re-troussage," and printers can produce strange effects by its use. A bad etching can be made to look like a good one; a good etching can be made to look weak and wretched. In fact, a clever artist printer can produce a capital picture from a plate which has nothing at all on it but the ink.

Etchings first appeared in English books about the end of the seventeenth century, but they are seldom signed, neither are they good. There is an etched frontispiece to Latroo's "English Roque," 1665, and another to "Æsop's Fables," published in the same year.

Wenceslaus Hollar, a Bohemian who worked in London, illustrated a few English books with etchings in the seventeenth century. Soft ground etchings printed in red and black appear in Pennant's "Account of London," printed in 1795. In the eighteenth and early nineteenth centuries William Blake made a few etchings for book illustrations. In the nineteenth century came Alken's etchings of animals, usually coloured, Samuel Hewitt, Doyle, and especially the excellent work of George Cruickshank, which was very much admired by John Ruskin.

Combined with line engraving a number of small illustrations were published in the nineteenth century. They were etched on steel, and carefully finished with small line work, with ruled skies. They are generally classed as engravings, but should, I think, rather be called etchings.

Etching has not played a very important part in French books any more than it has in English. There are the amusing sketches of Callot, good work by Abraham Bosse and Sebastian Leclerc, and in quite recent times the beautiful etchings by Jules Jacquemart of works of art, in their way unsurpassed, and marvels of technical skill. I have already mentioned a few French etchers who combined that work with small line engraving, probably on steel; of these probably Choffard is best known and most highly appreciated.

Engraving by dots has been for a long time practised, as by its means a graduated tone can be more easily obtained than it can by the use of line alone, and stipple is the same idea carried out by the etching needle instead of the graver.

Stipple is done by means of small bunches of needles, with which irregular dots are made in the etching ground and then bitten by acid, as usual. In most cases a few small finishing dots are put on the copper by hand afterwards. Stipple is excellent for faces, and is best known in the work of Bartolozzi, who excelled in it. It is said to have been invented by Jacob Bylaert, a Dutchman, in 1760.

Title-page of Grimm's "German Popular Stories." (London, 1824.)

Illustrated with etchings by George Cruickshank.

In England stipple engraving was largely used in the early nineteenth century for book illustrations. It is found chiefly in faces, and is generally supported by line engraving or etching. The best stipple engravers did not illustrate books, but the work of W. Finden, C. Knight, J. Parker, C. Marr, and W. Holl is always good, though, of course, very small. Besides these there were numbers of lesser stipple engravers, whose work is fair—Jenkinson, Dean, H. Cook, C. Wagstaffe, H. Robinson, and many more.

The same sort of usefulness was found for stipple abroad, for faces particularly, and it was successfully practised by Pfeiffer, Vangelisty, and others, but it never took the same hold upon the Continent that it did here, either in the case of small book illustrations or in the more important matter of large stipple engravings.

Mezzotints are not satisfactory if they are on a small scale. Delicate and minute work cannot be done well by the mezzotint process alone, but require supplementary line or etched work. So we find that mezzotints have not been much used for book illustration.

The process of mezzotinting was invented by Ludwig von Siegen, an officer in the Hessian Army, about 1642, and at first it was practised chiefly by foreigners, but it soon became the favourite method of engraving upon metal in England; indeed, the competition of the mezzotint eventually ruined the slower and more costly process of line engraving.

Some books concerning mezzotints have explanatory plates in them, beginning with Le Blon's "Coloritto," written about 1721, but these can hardly be considered as fair instances of ordinary book illustrations.

A copper plate is prepared for mezzotint engraving by being uniformly roughened all over, so that if it were inked and a print made from it, the print would show a uniform velvety black. The art of the "scraper" consists in so skilfully cutting away or burnishing down the roughened surface of the copper that when a print is made a picture appears. The scraper works from black to white whenever the surface is scraped or burnished away, so in exact correspondence the print will show grey or white. It is quick work, and easy work up to a point, but to make a first-rate mezzotint is a great art, and only a few engravers have succeeded in doing it.

Among the first students of the art was Prince Rupert, who was an excellent artist and an accomplished workman all round. He engraved a large plate after Spagnoletto, called "The Great Executioner," and when John Evelyn wrote a little book called "Sculptura," which was published in 1662, and included in it a short description of the new art, the Prince mezzotinted a plate for him, showing only the head of the great executioner. This head, the first mezzotint done for a book, is a finer piece of work than the head in the larger plate.

There were several anatomical plates, mostly printed in coloured inks, which were mezzotinted about the same time, but they are not important; then Faber's portraits of founders of the Colleges of Oxford and Cambridge were used as illustrations to Rolt's "Lives of the Reformers," published in 1759. These plates bear Houston's name as mezzotinter, but this is only one of a number of such re-letterings which occur in the history of mezzotints.

Robert Dunkarton engraved several book illustrations, mostly portraits, and he also helped in the mezzotinting of some of the plates in Turner's "Liber Studiorum." He was a portrait painter, and his mezzotints are better than Faber's. John

Young was an eminent mezzotinter, and in 1815 he issued a large book of portraits of the Emperors of Turkey printed in colours. They are not particularly good, but are interesting as being the first set of mezzotints to be issued in colour as book illustrations. The book is rare and, if the colour is strong, of considerable value.

Turner's "Liber Studiorum" was issued between 1807 and 1819, and many mezzotinters helped in the work—F. C. Lewis, Charles Turner, W. Say, R. Dunkarton, G. Clint, J. C. Eastling, T. Hodgetts, W. Annis, H. Dawe, T. Lipton, and S. W. Reynolds. The plates were not pure mezzotint, but were strongly etched as well with some aquatinting; the first etching was done by J. M. W. Turner, and some of the mezzotinting. I think he probably worked finally upon all the plates in various ways with burin, scraper and roulette.

Several books of landscapes are illustrated with mezzotints, done on copper or steel, by T. G. Lupton, many of them after Turner, and John Constable's landscapes have been admirably mezzotinted by David Lucas; perhaps the best known is "English Landscape Scenery," published in 1855.

In all mezzotints, large or small, it should be noted that the *condition* of the print is important. The blacks should be deep and velvety; if they show greyish or spotted, the print is from an old plate. Mezzotints on steel last better than if they are on copper. I know of no foreign books illustrated with mezzotints.

There are several ways of making aquatints, but the best is the oldest. It was invented by a Frenchman, J. B. Le Prince, towards the end of the eighteenth century, and although of foreign origin, the art has been most extensively and successfully practised in England.

Le Prince allowed powdered resin to settle evenly on a copper plate, fixed the minute grains by heat, and then treated the plate with acid as if it were an etching. When the plate was cleaned the acid is found to have bitten a little line round each grain of resin, so that an aquatint made by this method consists of a series of small rings more or less thick. The different thicknesses are produced by stopping out some portions and re-biting others. The general effect of aquatint is delicate and pleasing, and it can be strengthened where necessary with a little etching. Aquatint helps its followers considerably, and a good aquatint made from a drawing or painting will often have luminous effects that are wanting in the original.

There is one other method of aquatinting that must be mentioned, but there are more which are too numerous and too unimportant to require explanation here. It is a modern invention, and consists of coating the plate with resin dissolved in alcohol; when this dries it breaks up into little pieces, and the acid can penetrate between these pieces as in Le Prince's method. But the resulting prints do not show Le Prince's little circles, but small irregular polygons.

Le Prince sold his secret to Charles Greville, and he passed it on to Paul Sandby, who not only became an eminent aquatinter but published a book in 1775 called *Twelve Views in Aquatinta*. This drew much attention to the beautiful new art, and it rapidly became very popular in England. English aquatinters, like English wood and stipple engravers, always liked colour, whether added by hand or printed in ink, and so we find that the large majority of English aquatinters enjoy the added beauty of colour.

The publishers Ackermann and Boydell both deserve much honour for their consistent patronage of aquatints, and no doubt our splendid record in that art is largely due to their enterprise.

Towards the latter part of the eighteenth century we already find several fine books with hand-coloured aquatint illustrations published in England, among these are W. Hodge's *Select Views in India*, 1786; T. Hassell's *Picturesque Guide to Bath*, 1793; Combes' *History of the River Thames*, with aquatints by J. C. Stadler; E. Orme's *Twelve Views of Places in the Kingdom of Mysore*, with aquatints by J. W. Edy; and H. Repton's amusing *Sketches of Landscape Gardening*, with moveable plates to show how good his suggested improvements were, all published in 1794, and from this time for the next thirty years were numbers of books issued with coloured aquatints concerning domestic architecture.

Early in the nineteenth century there are still numbers of books with aquatint views in them: J. Webber's *Views in the South Seas*, published in 1808, and Boydell's *Picturesque Scenery of Norway*, with aquatints by J. W. Edy, in 1820, and several more.

Then Rowlandson, the caricaturist, aquatinted the illustrations for Goldsmith's *Vicar of Wakefield* in 1817, and the inimitable *Tour of Dr. Syntax*, by Combe, in 1820, thereby setting the fashion for caricature in aquatint, which had a considerable vogue.

In Pyne's *History of the Royal Residences*, the out-door views are printed in coloured inks, blue for the skies and brown for the foregrounds. They have additional hand-colouring. It is an important book, and was published in 1819; the aquatints are engraved by T. Sutherland, W. F. Bennett, R. Reeve, and others.

Then came a series of fine books on Indian scenery, mostly engraved by T. Medland, Hassell and Ellis, and many books of English views, mostly engraved by D. Havell, T. Sutherland, T. H. Fielding, J. Baily, or T. Cartwright.

Of less importance, but now becoming more esteemed, are the numbers of graceful costume and fashion plates which were done in aquatint and coloured by hand from about 1790 to 1840. These books are already much sought after, and will probably be more and more so in time; the plates are generally anonymous.

William Daniell illustrated Ayrton's *Voyage Round Great Britain* with beautiful coloured aquatints; it was published in 1825.

There are many cases in which several kinds of work appear on the same plate; there may be aquatint and etching, mezzotint with etching, engraving or aquatint, so it is very important to be able to judge from the aspect of a line or dot or a point by which method it has been produced.

The magnificent account of the *Coronation of George IV.*, published in 1825, under the care of Sir George Nayler, Garter King of Arms, is illustrated with mixed engravings, stipple, etching, line, aquatint and mezzotint, by S. W. Reynolds and other engravers, chiefly after designs by F. and J. Stephanoff. The plates are coloured by hand, and several of the special copies have much extra artistic work added. It is said to be the most expensive book ever published, and it never repaid its cost, but received a grant in aid from the Government of the day. The majority of the figures are careful portraits, and it is the highest authority for the State costume of the time.

Lithography is the art of drawing upon stone in such a way that prints can be made from the drawing. The drawing has to be done upon a particular sort of stone either directly or by means of transfer from lithographic paper, and it can be done either with a point of solid lithographic ink resembling black chalk, or by a liquid ink, in which case the drawing is called a lithotint. J. M. Whistler was remarkably successful in this latter manner, but it had been used long before by Hullmandel and Cattermole.

The discovery of lithography was due to the experiments of Aloys Senefelder, a native of Prague, who was born late in the eighteenth century. He accidentally found that some writing he had put on one of the stones he used for sharpening his tools upon came off easily on to paper or linen. Then he tried what effect acid would have, and found that it would eat away the stone wherever the ink did not prevent it, so he got a block in low relief. The protective ink is made essentially of wax, tallow, soap, shellac, and lamp black, and the acid renders this insoluble, so that when acid is applied to the stone the parts drawn upon remain unaffected. The drawing ink is now removed, and when printing ink is applied by means of a roller, it sticks only where the drawn lines are, and from this inked stone a print can be obtained.

The surface of a lithograph is quite smooth, and the process will not help an artist in the least—as the drawing is so will the lithograph from it be; the only difference is in the power of reproduction.

Senefelder was unfortunate; he introduced an art to the world which has been very largely followed, but his own efforts were failures from a business point of view. He came to London early in the nineteenth century, and his methods soon found votaries, but he shortly returned to Munich, where his brother had assisted him in setting up a lithographic establishment, and this practically failing, it was taken over by the Bavarian Government and put under the management of H. J. Mitterer, a professor of drawing.

But it was in France that lithography made most rapid progress. The clever French draughtsmen that happened to exist about that time very quickly mastered the process, and between them they established a school of lithography that is unequalled. Many of the greatest French artists worked in it, and some of them specialised in it.

Lasteyrie introduced it, and it was quickly taken up by Horace Vernet, Pierre Guerin, Charlet, and many others for small book illustrations, and about 1830 there are large numbers of caricatures done in this quick and easy way. Then Gericault, Henri Monnier, Eugène Delacroix, and J. B. Isabey swelled the list of French lithographers, most of the book illustrations being of small size; and a little later there is notable work done by Honoré Daumier, Achille Deveria, Raffet, Jean Gigoux and Gavarni, several of them specialising in military subjects. Towards the end of the century we find a new set of artists, many of whom use colour as well as monotint, Fantin-Latour, Chéret, O. Redon, Gandara and Willett.

The social side of French life is perhaps the most illustrated in lithography.

In England lithography received its first impetus from Senefelder himself, who came and worked in London, where in 1819 his *Complete Course of Lithography* was published.

C. J. Hullmandel and J. D. Harding were friends and co-workers in the new art, and they were both adepts at it; Hullmandel drew several of the beautiful plates of birds for John Gould, and they were afterwards coloured by hand. From the beginning colour has been much liked by English lithographers, either added by hand or produced by means of "chromo-lithography," that is, several plates inked in different colours and then printed over each other on one piece of paper.

Roberts' *Holy Land* is magnificently illustrated with lithographic plates by Louis Haghe, a left-handed Belgian, who worked here, and these plates were afterwards coloured by hand. Clarkson Stanfield and Cattermole both worked in lithography, and Nash's *Mansions of England in the Olden Time*, 1839-49, are familiar to most of us. Nash coloured several copies by hand.

Owen Jones' *Plans of the Alhambra*, published 1842-5, are excellent chromo-lithographs. In quite modern times the old tradition is worthily upheld by William Griggs, whose colour plates of *Illuminated MSS. in the British Museum* are in every way excellent—indeed, for truth and fidelity to their originals they have never been equalled.

Munich was a sort of headquarters of lithography in the early part of the nineteenth century, when H. J. Mitterer succeeded to Senefelder's establishment there. Among the first lithographers in Germany were J. M. Mittenleiter, who also invented the art of engraving on stone, and Joseph Hauber.

Most of the German lithographers contented themselves with making copies of existing pictures, and one of the finest examples of this kind of lithography is to be found in the *Gemälde Galerie des K. Museums in Berlin*, published in 1842, and containing excellent work by Fr. Jentzen, C. Fischer, and others.

Adolf Menzel did some notable lithographic work about the middle of the century, and Mouilleron, Eybl, and Ritter were all excellent workmen.

Belgian lithographers have nearly always been very good; besides Haghe, who worked in England, there were, with others, Tuerlinckoe, Van der Meulen, and Van Loo.

Although there have been lithographic workshops set up at Rome, Florence, Turin, Milan, and other towns, the art has never flourished much in Italy: it never appealed to the sensitive artistic Italian nature. Such examples as do exist are mostly portraits.

Lithography has been popular in Spain, and Spanish artists have done excellent work in this manner.

In 1824 J. de Madrazo published the most important Spanish work illustrated with photographs; it is called *Collection lithographica de cuadros del Rey ... Fernando VII., lithographiada por habiles artistas*, among whom are named J. Jollivet, P. Blanchard and A. Guerrero. The work of all of these is excellent. Lithographic work in Spain, so far as books are concerned, has been mostly of an archæological character—views of old buildings or old pictures particularly. F. Goya, however, worked largely in this manner.

All these methods of illustrating books worked by hand have now been superseded by one or other of the wonderful processes made possible by the invention of photography. Some of these are expensive, but generally they are cheap.

The most elaborate, and when well done the most wonderful, of these processes is that known as heliogravure. By means of this method reproductions of line engravings can be made so perfectly that detection is almost impossible. A metal plate is so treated by help of a photographic negative that the lines of the engraving are deposited in an insoluble form upon the plate, which is otherwise clean, then a thin film of metal is deposited on all the clean places by means of electrotyping, so that when the lines are dissolved out, they are in intaglio, just as they were in the original engraved plate. From this artificial plate prints can be made as if from an engraved plate.

For the mezzotint another method is adopted, known as photogravure, and this is also a wonderful invention. A metal plate is slightly roughed—if it could be more roughed it would be better—and then a photographic relief in gelatine is put upon it and etched. The result is a plate resembling a fine grain mezzotint, but the prints made from it are always deficient in the blacks. To remedy this and other defects which at present seem to be inherent, an engraver generally goes over the plate with roulette and burnisher. The Photogravure has ruined the Mezzotint. The coating of the copper-plates with steel largely adds to their life.

Then we come to the wood engravings, which are all perfectly imitated by the zinc block, made directly from the original drawing, and set on a wood block so as to range exactly with type in height. Wash drawings are closely copied by the half-tone process, which is also used with blocks that can be printed with type. The drawing to be copied is photographed through a glass screen very finely etched with minute lines crossing each other, so that the picture is ultimately represented by a series of little squares, black or white according to the tones of the original. But the whites are never quite satisfactory, the dots of the screen always show a little, so the dispossessed wood engraver has to be called in after all to touch them up with a graver. In America, where the half-tone process has reached a very high degree of excellence, the names of these helpful engravers are frequently added. A curious "shot-silk" effect is often seen in half-tone illustrations where the lines of the screen fall at a particular angle with the lines on the original. The same peculiarity sometimes shows in the ruled sky lines in the small nineteenth century line engravings.

The three-colour process consists of half-tone blocks printed in colours one over the other, but although they look well they are not particularly true to their originals. The reason of this is that each block is a little wrongly inked, as the tint of the pigment put upon it depends entirely upon the printer. He has of course a carefully coloured key given him to match for each block, but he never quite succeeds in doing more than get near it. There are line keys and colour blocks, and half-tone and colour blocks, and many other varieties of combinations of processes.

The half-tone process is certainly responsible for much charming and valuable work, but it has done one very great harm not only to itself but even to literature, it has been the chief cause of the introduction of clay-laden paper (see Chap. III.).

The beauty of photographic illustrations can be best seen in some of the recent French illustrated books in colour published by the Société des Amis des Livres. Other exquisite illustrations are to be found in Octave Uzanne's books, many of them from the drawings of Paul Avril. The way in which many of these illustrations are made to show over the printed page is often quite charming.

BOOKS TO CONSULT.

BAER, L.—Die Illustrirten Historienbücher des 15 Jahrhunderts. *Strassburg*, 1903.

BAYARD, E.—Illustrations et les Illustrateurs. *Paris*, 1898.

BLACKBURN, H.—The Art of Illustration. *London*, 1896-1901.

BONNET, G.—Manuel de Phototypie. *Paris*, 1889.

BONNET, G.—Manuel d'Héliogravure et de Photogravure en relief. *Paris*, 1890.

BOUCHOT, H.—Le Livre, L'Illustration. *Paris*, 1886.

BOUCHOT, H.—Les Livres a vignettes. *Paris*.

BRIVOIS, J.—Bibliographie des livres a gravures sur bois du XIXe siècle. *Paris*, 1883.

BROUGH, W. S.—Book Illustration. *Leek*, 1891.

BULLOCK, J. M.—Art of Extra Illustration. 1903.

CRANE, W.—Of the Decorative Illustration of Books. *London*, 1901.

DAVENPORT, CYRIL.—Mezzotints. *London*, 1904.

DOBSON, A.—(Chapter on Illustrated Books in Lang's "The Library.") *London*, 1881.

DOBSON, H. A.—Bewick and his Pupils. *London*, 1884.

DUCHOCHOIS, P. C.—Photographic Reproduction Processes. *London*, 1892.

FARQUHAR, H. D.—Grammar of Photo-engraving. *London*, 1895.

GERRING, C.—Notes on Book Illustration. *Nottingham*, 1898.

GEYMET, T.—Traité de Gravure en demi-teint par l'invention du cliché photographique. *Paris*, 1888.

GEYMET, T.—Traité de Gravure et impression sur zinc. *Paris*, 1887.

GEYMET, T.—Traité de Photogravure. *Paris*, 1886.

Geymet, T.—Traité de Photo-lithographie. *Paris*, 1888.

Grolier Club, New York.—Catalogue of Engraved Titles and Frontispieces published in England during the sixteenth and seventeenth centuries. *New York*, 1898.

Hardie, M.—English Coloured Books. *London*, 1906.

Henrich, M.—Iconographie de las ediciones del Quijote de M. de Cervantes Saavedra. *Barcelona*, 1905.

Hinton, A. H.—Handbook of Illustration. *London*, 1895-1905.

Hodson, J. S.—Guide to Art Illustration. *London*, 1884.

Huson, T.—Photo-Aquatint. *London*, 1897.

Jackson, J. B.—An essay on engraving in Chiaro Oscuro. *London*, 1754.

Kirkbridge, J.—Engraving for Illustrations. *London*, 1903.

Kristeller, P.—Early Florentine Woodcuts. *London*, 1897.

Kristeller, P.—Die Strassburgher Bucher-illustration im XV. und XVI. Jahrhunderts. *Leipzig*, 1888.

Lietze, E.—Modern Heliographic Processes. *New York*, 1888.

Linton, W. J.—The Masters of Wood Engraving. *New Haven, Conn.*, 1889.

Linton, W. J.—Wood Engraving in America. *London*, 1881.

Madrazo, J. de.—Collection lithografica cuadros del Rey ... Fernando VII. 1824.

Martineau, R.—The Mainz Psalter of 1457 (Bibliographica, Vol. I.).

Massena, A. P. V.—Etudes sur l'art de la gravure sur bois a Venise. *Paris*, 1895-6.

Morin, L.—French Illustrators. *New York*, 1893.

Muther, R.—Die deutsche Bücherillustration. *Leipzig*, 1884.

Papillon, J. B. M.—Traité de la gravure en bois. *Paris*, 1766.

Pennell, J.—The Illustration of Books. *London*, 1896.

Pennell, J.—Modern Illustration. *London*, 1895.

Pennell, J., and E. R.—Lithography and Lithographers. *London*, 1898.

Pingrenon, R.—Les livres ornés et illustrés en couleur depuis le XVᵉ Siècle en France et en Angleterre.

Pollard, A. W.—Early Illustrated Books. *London*, 1893.

Pollard, A. W.—Italian Book Illustrations. *London*, 1894.

Roux, V.—Traité de gravure héliographique en taille douce. *Paris*, 1886.

Schnauss, J.—Collotype and Photo-lithography. *London*, 1889.

Senefelder.—Complete Course of Lithography. *London*, 1879.

SINGER, H. W., and STRANG, W.—Etching, Engraving, etc. *London*, 1897.

SKETCHLEY, R. E. D.—English Book Illustration of To-day. *London*, 1903.

SMITH, F. H.—American Illustrators. *New York*, 1893.

STRANGE, E. F.—Japanese Illustration. *London*, 1897.

VERFASSER, J.—The Half-tone Process. *London*, 1904.

VIDAL, L.—Traité Pratique de Photo-lithographie. *Paris*, 1893.

VILLON, A. M.—Traité Pratique de Photogravure. *Paris*, 1891.

WHITE, J. W. G.—English Illustration, "The Sixties." *Westminster*, 1897.

WIESBACH, W.—Die Baseler Buchillustration des XV. Jahrhunderts. *Leipzig*, 1896.

WILKINSON, W. T.—Photo-mechanical Processes. *London*, 1892.

WOOD, H. T.—Modern Methods of Illustrating Books. *London*, 1887.

CHAPTER VI.

MISCELLANEA.

Book edges and their decoration—Embroidered books—Cloth bindings—Account books—End papers—Small metal-bound books—
Books bound in tortoiseshell—Chained books—Horn books.

The projecting bosses and corners which occur in mediæval bindings were to
protect them against the friction of other books which lay upon them, a thin piece
of wood dividing them. The books were piled upon each other, so that if one of the
lower ones was wanted it was necessary to remove the upper ones. This caused
much trouble, so that in due time it was found better to stand the books up on end
on shelves.

The prone position is, however, the better one for the book, and the respective
levels of the edges of the book and the edges of the boards are designed for this
position. When the books were set up on end, the discrepancy between the levels
of the book edges and the board edges was never rectified, and the result is that a
large amount of damage has been done. When a large book is set up on end, the
weight of it rests entirely upon the lower edges of the boards, and the lower edges
of the book itself are up in the air above the shelf by so much as the projection of
the edges of the boards beyond them. The result is that the whole of the weight of
the vellum or paper of the book pulls upon the bands of the back in their weakest
direction, from within and more particularly from the top, thereby pulling the
back inwards. The mass of the book falls forward slantingly, until the lower edge
of the front of it rests upon the shelf.

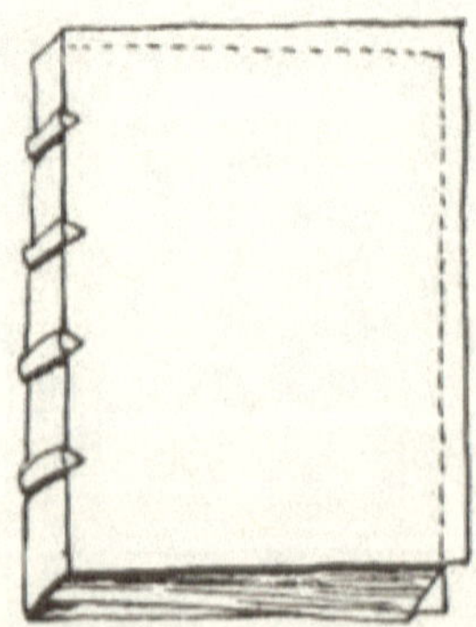

Fig. 70.—Inside of heavy book fallen forward, by reason of being kept upright.

It is difficult to describe, but my sketch will show what I mean, and the truth of it can be easily seen in almost any library of old books that are kept "on end"; the edges will be found grubby from resting on the shelf, and the top of the back will be found pulled forward.

Valuable books that are kept upright should have the edges of the boards level with the edges of the leaves, and then this disastrous pull would not occur.

A remedy, however, may be found by means of a piece of wood cut the same size as the lower edge of the book so as to fit closely into the hollow between the outer edges of the boards and the lower edges of the leaves. Such a slip will neutralise the drop of the leaves, and preserve the proper form of the backs of heavy books.

But before the upright position was finally adopted for books, and their titles were put on their backs, the front edge or "forage" of the leaves was always kept outwards, in view, and on this space or long panel all sorts of devices and letterings were put.

Leaves of a book, pressed tightly together, provided too tempting a space to be ignored, to say nothing of the usefulness of giving the name or title of the book, or the device of its owner, or even a decorative design. So on fine mediæval books and also on later books, following the earlier manner in their own way, we find all sorts of designs on book edges. It is not a subject which has attracted much attention as yet, but it probably will in time, and there is already enough known about it to show that much valuable knowledge is lying hidden up in it. For instance, if a book, otherwise likely, has the words "Rex in Æternum Vive" painted in gold on the edges, it is a positive sign that it issued from the workshop of Thomas Berthelet, printer and binder to Henry VIII.

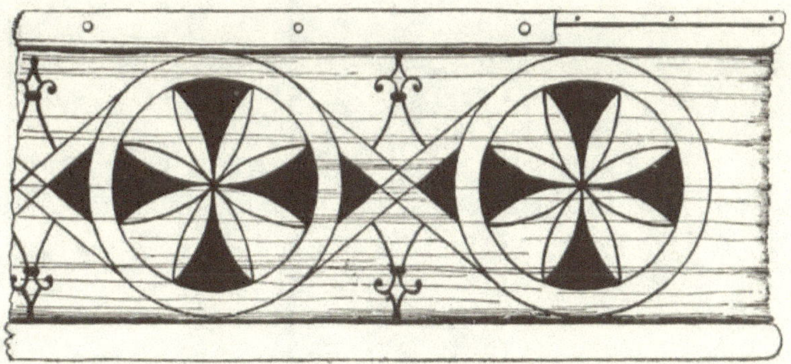

Fig. 71.—Forage decoration in colour. Tenth century.

Edge decoration of some sort seems to have been done from the tenth century onwards; at first elementary or symbolical designs were simply painted upon the edges, and not counting the mere book titles or press marks, it may be said that since the fourteenth century heraldry has played a very important part in edge decoration. In England this form of adornment for a bound book has been largely followed from that time, and there are fine examples of it in books bound for

Henry VII. and the other of our Tudor sovereigns, as well as for private persons of the same period. The edges are treated as panels and the painting done upon them when pressed firmly and solidly together. The edges are generally coloured some neutral colour as a groundwork and sometimes lettering in gold is done upon them.

Fig. 72.—Italian forage decoration in gold and colour (1560).

Fig. 73.—German forage decoration in gold and colour.
The arms of Nuremberg (1566).

Henry VIII. often had the legend "Rex in Æternum Vive Nez" written in gold on the cream coloured edges of his books, and all that are so lettered are attributed to Thomas Berthelet as binder. The "Nez" is rather a puzzle, and it was suggested by Mr. J. L. Scott, of the British Museum, that it stands for the three initial letters of the phrase in the Book of Daniel, Ναβουχοδονόσωϱ Εσαει ζῆθι—a quite possible solution.

Queen Anne Boleyn's copy of the New Testament has her name, "Anna Regina Angliæ," written in red upon its gilt edges.

For Queen Elizabeth, book edges were usually gilded, and on this gilding designs were impressed with ordinary binding tools. This is the commonest form of edge decoration, and is called "gauffring." Gauffred edges are found in abundance in French, German and Italian work. There are fine examples of it on books bound for Henri II. of France and all his children, and on those made for Diane de Poictiers, Duchesse de Valentinois. In all these cases colour is often added to the designs on the gold. Le Gascon put some elaborately painted edges on some of his hooks; on Italian books and English books colour is sparingly used; on the other hand, in Germany and the Low Countries colour was often overdone and the result is garish.

Until the time of Samuel Mearne, towards the end of the seventeenth century, all edge paintings were done on the edges of the leaves simply pressed solidly together, but Mearne invented a new fashion of arranging the leaves. In the case of the older manner we usually find the upper and lower edges painted as well as the fore-edge, or "forage," but it is only the forage that can be painted in Mearne's style, and so in all instances of this kind the upper and lower edges are left plain.

Fig. 74.—Book fanned out to show forage painting in Mearne's style.

Mearne had his book forwarded, finished, and the edges gilded before beginning his painting. Then he opened the book by the upper board only, and laid it down flat on its back and kept it in that position by weights. In this position it will be found that the forage fans out into a larger panel than exists when the book is shut up. On this fanned-out panel the painting was done in water-colours with as dry a brush as possible. When the painting was finished and the book allowed to resume its normal shut position, the edge painting entirely disappeared, and the gilding on the forage looked as if nothing was behind it. So thoroughly does such a painting disappear that I have found several that were quite unknown to their owners, and I have no doubt that there are plenty of unrecognised examples in English private libraries in perfect condition and safe obscurity.

Fig. 75.—Portrait of Charles II. in colour, on the forage of a book bound for the king by Samuel Mearne.

The only name I have found on any of Mearne's forage paintings is that of "Fletcher."

After Mearne, for about one hundred years, I know of no particular development of forage decoration, but towards the end of the eighteenth century, the same principle was revived by James Edwards of Halifax. Edwards had an artist brother, and it is likely enough that he painted the edges on his brother's curious vellum-bound books. The designs are not so markedly heraldic as the earlier examples were, but are often biblical.

Edwards' delicate paintings, always on small books, were copied for some considerable period, and many little books were made with such work upon them for many years. Windsor and Eton are both favourite subjects, and country houses of all sorts. Landscapes are particularly suitable for this form of painting, and many specimens are very pleasing.

All the foregoing paintings are done so as to be complete on each book, but some time ago a remarkable set of Italian books, I believe of the sixteenth century, were brought to England. The forages of these volumes were painted in such a manner that the complete design only showed when they were all arranged in proper order on a shelf with their forages outwards. In the case of sets of books bound uniformly, this manner of ornamenting them is worthy of the attention of some of our enterprising modern binders.

Although the greater number of books, both in manuscript and printed, have been bound in leather or vellum, there are still very many that have been covered in other materials.

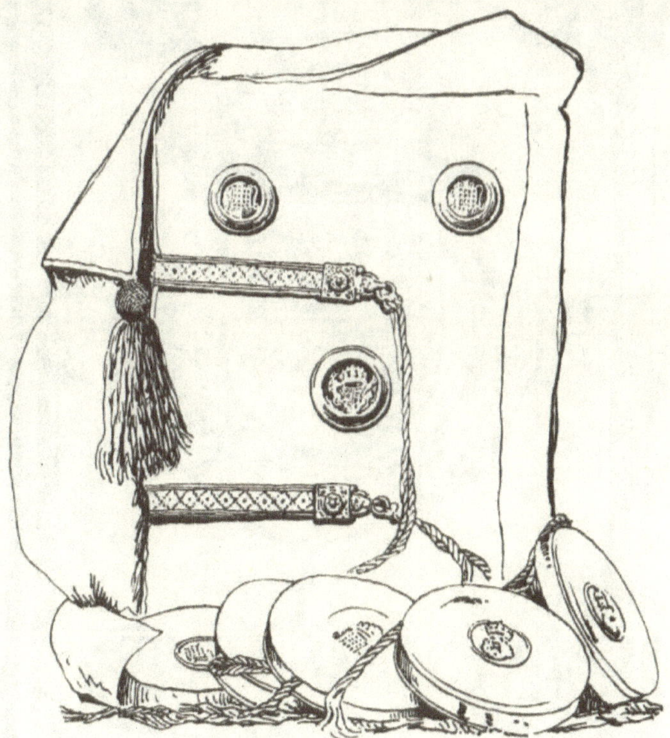

Fig. 76.—English velvet binding, with seals, made for Henry VII.

The commonest of these materials are velvet, canvas, satin, silk, cloth, linen, and buckram. I believe that all of these, except perhaps the last three in recent times, have been more used in England than they have been in any other country.

Velvet is the most interesting, as its use is the most ancient, of any of these textile materials. It is strong and beautiful, the fur or pile being produced in a very curious manner. Two warps are used in the manufacture of the fabric, and small hollow brass wires, slightly flattened at the sides, and having a groove along the top, are inserted transversely under the raised "pile" warp at intervals as the weaving proceeds. These wires keep the thread in the form of upright loops, resembling those which can be seen on a Brussels carpet on a larger scale. The wires are then cut out by drawing a sharp specially-designed knife called a truvat along the groove at the top. The consequent separation of the warp threads which formed the rows of loops now forms the pile, each thread standing upright. It is wonderful how well velvet lasts, and what hard wear it will stand before all the pile is worn away.

Fig. 77.—English embroidered book, velvet. Made for Henry VIII.

Books bound in velvet are not uncommon in Dutch work; they are sometimes inlaid in differently coloured velvets, and sometimes embroidered. In France books have rarely been bound in velvet, in Italy and in Germany still more rarely.

In England, however, there has been a considerable output of velvet bindings. Examples still exist that were made in the fifteenth century for Henry VII., whose library was in all probability entirely bound in this material. Nothing earlier than Henry VII.'s books are now known of English bindings in velvet, but these are so fine that it is likely enough that earlier work of the kind was done in the case of very choice manuscripts.

Not only are Henry VII.'s books, which are still in their original covers, in marvellously good condition, but they are also among the most decorative bindings that have ever been made, here or in any other country. Fine examples may be seen in the library at Westminster Abbey, at the Record Office, and in the British Museum, and in every case their beauty and interest well repay the trouble of obtaining access to them.

These volumes all are in the same style, but they vary in detail. All I have seen are in red velvet, and have metal bosses in the centre and smaller ones in the corner.

One of the handsomest, which may be taken as a type, is a copy of the indentures made between Abbot Islip and Henry VII. for the foundation of the chantry at Westminster. It is a large manuscript on vellum, and is covered in rich red velvet projecting liberally over the edges, and bound with gold fringe. In the centre is a circular silver cup-like boss, containing the royal coat of arms, France and England quarterly, with supporters of red dragon of Cadwallader and white greyhound of De Beaufort, cut out of silver and enamelled in proper colours. At each corner is a circular silver boss containing the De Beaufort device of a portcullis gilt and cut in low relief, and set on an enamelled background of the Tudor livery colours, green and white, per pale. There are clasps of cloth of gold braid, fastening with a chased silver-gilt button bearing an enamelled rose, and dependent from the lower edge of the board are five silver boxes bearing Tudor emblems in relief, each containing an impression of the great seal.

It is also recorded by Paul Hentzner that in 1598 he saw Queen Elizabeth's library, and that many of them were bound in velvet and embroidered, a note that is fully corroborated by such of her books as now remain.

But there were also books embroidered upon canvas in the fifteenth century, one of which is now in the British Museum. It is a psalter of the fourteenth century, and is covered in fine canvas on which are delicate embroideries in the manner known as "Opus Anglicanum," which looks like a chain stitch, but is really a cleverly managed split stitch.

This remarkable book, the earliest known example of an embroidered binding, has upon one side a beautiful representation of the Annunciation, and on the other a Crucifixion. It is supposed to have been worked by Anne de Felbrigge, a nun in the convent of Minoresses, at Brusyard, in Suffolk, and daughter of Sir Simon de Felbrigge, K.G., standard bearer to Richard II. It is considerably worn and faded, but the designs can all be made out.

The velvet books which were made in the next reign were ornamented with embroidered designs appliqués, and many of them are very handsome. The designs on such books were nearly always heraldic, judging from those that remain, but arabesques and floral ornamentation are often met with on satin. Queen Katharine Parr is said to have embroidered some of these books, and there is one in canvas in the British Museum, and one in canvas and one in velvet at the Bodleian, which are supposed to have been worked by the Princess Elizabeth, always with braid.

Fig. 78.—English embroidered book, canvas (1648).

When Elizabeth came to the throne she continued her evident liking for velvet bound books, and she had them of several colours—red, green, or black. Several of these are richly embroidered, sometimes with armorial designs, sometimes floral, and sometimes arabesque. Others are decorated with brilliant enamels or gold, centrepieces, cornerpieces, and clasps, and others again have appliqué pieces of coloured satin, on which is gold tooling, some of which is actually put on the velvet itself.

Canvas is rarely found during Elizabeth's reign, but it does exist, and is usually embroidered in a coarse manner with tent-stitch.

In the seventeenth century the taste for velvet bindings still remained, but not so exclusively, as there were many more bound in silk or satin, usually white. The majority of these books are small, Prayers, Bibles, Psalms, and the designs upon them are of great variety, but generally have a symbolic tendency—figures of Faith, Hope, Charity, Peace, Plenty, and numbers of biblical subjects, David and Bathsheba, Solomon and Queen of Sheba, Jacob's Dream, Jacob wrestling with the Angel, Abraham and Isaac, and many more; and besides these there are numbers of quaint little bindings with floral designs.

Fig. 79.—English embroidered "double" book, satin, seventeenth century.

The period of Nicholas Ferrar's curious establishment at Little Gidding in Huntingdonshire was coincident with the reign of Charles I. Here were contrived most interesting Harmonies of the Scriptures, done under Ferrar's superintendence by his nieces Mary Collet and her sisters. These ladies, moreover, bound the Harmonies themselves, and were not only the first English lady binders but also the first amateur binders, and they bound exceedingly well. Mrs. Wordsworth was another pioneer among lady binders. She covered her books in pieces of her own old dresses.

Not only did the ladies of Little Gidding bind their Harmonies, sometimes very large, in sheep skin, morocco and calf, but also in velvet, curiously ornamented. I have already mentioned that in the sixteenth century the art of gilding upon velvet was known, but it was reserved for the ladies of Little Gidding to bring it to perfection.

Fig. 80.—English, embroidered binding canvas, seventeenth century.

There will always be some little doubt as to whether these magnificent gold and silver tooled velvet books were done entirely by the binders at Little Gidding, or with the assistance of their masters, Bucks of Cambridge. There is a marked similarity of general style as well as of detail, but the larger Little Gidding books appear particularly to bear the impress of more irresponsible genius than that of the orthodox university printers.

Gilding upon velvet is still practised a little in England; the service books used at the wedding of the present Prince of Wales were in red velvet with the royal monogram impressed in gold upon it.

With the eighteenth century an end came to any great output of bindings in velvet, canvas or satin; now and then an isolated specimen is found, and the era of cloth bindings began in the nineteenth century.

The main difference is that the earlier books in velvet, canvas or satin were always specially broad, but the cloth bindings were trade bindings from the beginning, with very few exceptions.

At first backs of paper bound books were strengthened by pieces of ordinary linen or calico pasted over them, the title being added on a label; but a special cloth for binding purposes was made early in the century by James Leonard Wilson, and in 1822 Pickering's Aldine Classics bound in that material were issued. This use of a special cloth was largely helped and fostered by Mr. Archibald Leighton, who made a speciality of it. The cloth was sometimes watered and sometimes plain. Cloth soon became a favourite binding for cheap books, and in time Wilson found a way of gilding upon it, probably by the use of dried and powdered albumen.

Some of the early cloth bindings were ornamented by impressions from engraved cylinders, the pattern showing in low relief. The great pressure which was used to make this impression had so hardened the cloth as well as the boards upon which it is fixed, that many of the existing examples of the work are still in perfect condition.

Then gradually came ornamentation stamped in gold on the sides and gold lettering on the back, and of recent years designs and pictures stamped in colours upon cloth, canvas and buckram have become common. Many of these designs are excellent, and the work required for them gives employment to a large number of designers as well as colour printers and block makers. Books bound in these materials look well and last well for a time, but they are essentially short-lived if handled much.

About the middle of the nineteenth century numbers of small illustrated periodicals, landscape annuals, and the like were covered in watered silk, generally red, blue or green. These also do not last well; but if any copies that are still in a good state are found, they should be carefully preserved as they are, and not be rebound; they represent a type of binding that is by no means without charm. Perhaps the most important books which were originally issued in this form of cover were the two beautiful volumes of Rogers' *Poems* and *Italy*. They have gilt edges and are bound with flat open backs and sawn in bands.

Buckram is generally used for large books, as it is stiff and troublesome to fold over in a small way. If a large book is properly sewn and has proper boards it may well be covered in buckram, provided it is not to be much used. The joints soon look unsightly, as the hinge movement causes the dressing, of which there is a large proportion, to powder out. Buckram is rarely ornamented; indeed, it may almost be said that a book bound in it is only intended to keep together until such time as it can be properly bound in some better material.

Art canvas is sometimes used for bindings, and it is fairly satisfactory, but has the same delicacy at the joints as buckram, and soon looks shabby.

There is now such a quantity of cheap literature that is not likely to last, or to be wanted to last, that there is a large and increasing demand for cheap binding materials other than leather. So there is an important future for specially prepared binding cloths and buckrams. The only libraries that are likely to suffer by the more general introduction of such materials are the few large ones that are obliged to keep all their books, old or new, in working order inside and outside.

Account book bindings are peculiar and very strong. They have been used for a long time in banks and business houses, and are purely utilitarian and comparatively quite modern.

Strong sound paper is an essential for account books. The sewing is done in the flexible style, but on broad flat bands of vellum or leather instead of raised bands of hemp. The ends of the bands are fixed between two boards, pairs of which form the boards of the book. The space between the edge of the back of the book where the bands leave it and their inset to the boards is not drawn close, but a narrow margin is left so that a perfectly flexible and strong leather joint is left. In small books this peculiarity is known as a French joint, and it obviates the common failing of sides falling away from otherwise sound bindings along the joint-line at the back.

The back of account book bindings looks very strong, but it is really nothing of the sort. It is only a show back, to take the lettering and cover up the real joints, which are securely laid along the edges of the boards.

When an account book is opened it "sets up" so that it can be easily read right down to the sewing at the back. This is of great value in many cases other than the keeping of accounts, and it is the only advantage of the common, but weak, bindings with "hollow" backs. But there is no doubt that a modified form of account book binding, with a French joint, is a style which might with advantage be studied by our modern art binders.

The study of end papers is to some extent necessary for the true judgment of the work of certain binders. For instance, Thomas Berthelet normally used white end papers, Samuel Mearne used red marbled end papers, and Roger Payne used purple or pink end papers. The Italian binder who worked for Grolier used vellum for end paper, and so on. The knowledge of such details is useful in detecting frauds, as they are apt to be under-estimated in importance by a forger.

Of all end papers the most common is marbled paper, and one of the most curious usages of it is when a beautiful and delicate French binding has a charmingly gold tooled doublure of splendid leather faced by a wretched leaf of marbled paper.

The usual marbled paper is made by means of a bed of size on which colour is sprinkled by a brush, the colour lies on the top of the size and is moved about by means of a wide-toothed comb or a pin or anything that is handy, until the resulting pattern is to the satisfaction of the operator. Then the paper is laid down in the size, and when raised up it brings all the colour with it. It is generally easy to see how the pattern has been made by looking at the paper, and it will be found that the most usual forms have been made by the use of a broad-toothed comb. I should think that the process might well have produced something better than it ever has; undoubtedly if J. M. Whistler had ever known of it we should have had some remarkable results.

Marbling is probably of Oriental origin, and was most likely first practised in Germany, so far as Europe is concerned. It was certainly understood in Nuremberg in 1599, as specimens made there are to be seen in the *Album Amicorum*, of J. Cellarius, of that date. It is, of course, obviously capable of endless modifications, and of late years some very delicately and prettily coloured end papers have been made.

More or less in continuation of the mediæval fashion of covering book-bindings with richly-worked metal overlays, we find, in the seventeenth and eighteenth centuries particularly, numbers of small books bound in metal or with metal enrichments in the form of centrepieces and cornerpieces. Clasps occur all along, and although I hardly think that they have followed out any very marked line of development, I expect that some day a careful study will be made of them, when some such development may possibly be discovered. No student, as far as I am aware, has made any attempt to classify book clasps.

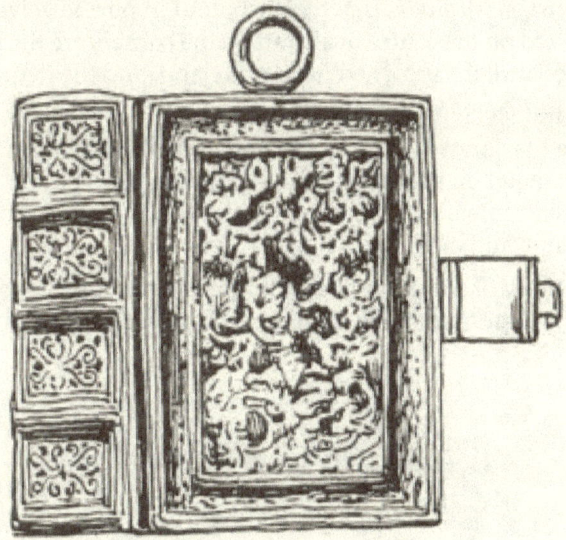

Fig. 81.—English golden book, made for Henry VIII.

But the English, German, French, Italian, and Dutch bindings with metal enrichments are pretty well known and generally admired. The English are the finest by far, and, as far as I can ascertain, the earliest. In the reign of Henry VIII. it was the fashion for ladies to carry small books of devotion at their girdle. These little books were always ornamental, and they had a ring fixed on the lower edge of the binding so that when the book was lifted up it came right for reading. One of these belonged to one of the queens of Henry VIII.; it is a copy of the Psalms, and is bound in gold with a delicate leafy spray in high relief. On it are remains of enamel, and in the beginning is a tiny miniature of the king.

Another beautiful little golden book with a design, probably by Holbein, in black enamel, is now the property of Lord Romney.

Several small golden bindings with scriptural subjects in high relief and enamelled were made late in the sixteenth century. Most of these are now divorced from their original texts, and are only kept as specimens of enamel work, but in one instance the whole book is perfect. This is a little book of prayers that belonged to Queen Elizabeth. On one side of it is the Serpent in the Wilderness and on the other the Judgment of Solomon.

For the same queen a little copy of *Christian Meditations* was bound in red velvet with golden centrepieces, corners, and clasps. The enamels in this case are champlevé, and still perfect in colour. They are said to have been the work of George Heriot, Elizabeth's goldsmith, who founded a hospital in Edinburgh.

James VI. of Scotland wrote the βασιλικον Δωρον for his son Henry, and the precious MS. was bound in purple velvet with golden centrepiece and clasps. The gold is cut out thin and then finished by engraving. When king of England James had some of his books bound in velvet with silver enrichments. On one of these, a little book of *Christian Meditations*, which is bound in purple velvet, the royal coat-of-arms is engraved on the centre oval, and on the corners are the national crests of England and Scotland, the crowned harp of Ireland, and the fleur-de-lis of France.

A beautiful little New Testament of 1643 with silver portraits of Charles I. and Queen Henrietta Maria, and cornerpieces and clasps engraved with allegorical figures, shows that metal on velvet was still a popular style, but on later bindings in England metal centrepieces fell quite out of use. Metal corners, however, were still used for some time, and clasps occasionally.

Bindings entirely of silver are rare in English workmanship, but they were not unknown, as a fine specimen with a repoussé figure of Charity covers a Common Prayer of 1632.

Fig. 82.—German binding in silver filigree and niello.

Of German and Dutch workmanship many metal bindings exist, and they are of varied styles. All these bindings have solid metal backs with hinges along the sides, and usually a sort of cap projecting over the headband. Many of the later examples are not good, but are made of bad metal and coarsely worked in repoussé. The worst of them are probably Dutch work.

Some of the earlier German silver bindings are prettily ornamented with niello work, and others have filigree work over gilt metal, and the use of tortoiseshell with silver or gilt mounts is also found of Spanish, German, or Dutch workmanship. I should say that the best guide to determine to which of these countries the work belongs is to take the place of imprint as authoritative. The imprint on a printed book does not by any means always imply that a binding was made there, but in many doubtful cases it is undoubtedly of much value as to mere nationality; the style of the binding itself should always be the first consideration. Some Dutch bindings are made in base metal, gilt, often with open work and engraving. They are neither good to look upon nor pleasant to handle.

Italian bindings in metal are rare, and it is only in the case of very small books that it was ever used. The manner of this is usually fine filigree work over a gilt groundwork. There is one example in the Victoria and Albert Museum, which is, however, more likely to be quite an exceptional production than one in any way representing a national type. It is an exquisitely enamelled golden book cover, having on one side the Garden of Eden and on the other the Fountain of Youth; it contains a missal, and is said to have been made for Queen Henrietta Maria.

Fig. 83.—Dutch binding in tortoiseshell and silver.

In France a few silver bindings of the sixteenth century with enamels have been made, but they are very rare, and the enamels of the basse taille style, usually badly chipped.

I believe some small metal bindings with rough enamels upon them have been made in comparatively modern times in Russia. These all have a strong Byzantine feeling and are clear survivals of the same style that was in vogue in Russia in mediæval times, and was used not only for bindings but also for ikons and triptychs. The work is coarse and unsatisfactory.

Tortoiseshell mounted in metal has been largely used for bindings in Holland, Germany, and Spain. The backs are hinged to the sides with long snuff-box hinges, and the shell itself is sometimes beautifully inlaid with silver and mother-of-pearl. Some of these covers are very small, particularly the Dutch ones, and designs are sometimes impressed upon them.

Mother-of-pearl has now and then been utilised for binding very small books. The backs and hinges are usually of silver.

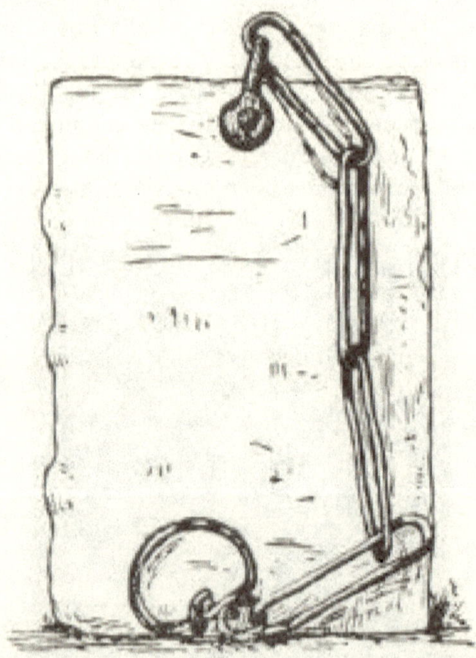

Fig. 84.—German chained book, fifteenth century.

The curious custom of fastening books to their shelves by means of chains was common enough in Europe in mediæval times and became almost universal in the sixteenth and seventeenth centuries in churches. It was of course done as a safeguard against thieves, and as far as I know only in the case of printed books. Although printed books soon became plentiful, yet no doubt in the case of Bibles and Prayer Books it is likely enough that a considerable leakage took place. Such small books were commonly chained to the backs of the pews in private chapels throughout England, and undoubtedly the custom, though inconvenient in use, was effective enough for its purpose.

Larger books would naturally belong to important libraries, those of cathedrals and churches particularly, and of these there are still left plenty of examples still in chains.

The chains are of iron, average 3 feet long, and are clamped to the front edge of the upper board by means of a rivet; the other end of the chain is provided with a ring which runs freely to and fro along a locked metal rod. Enough play is given by the chain to allow of the book being taken off its shelf and rested on the desk close at hand which is always provided for it.

There is a certain fashion in the way of attaching these chains. In foreign books the fastening is usually found at the top of the upper board, while in the case of English books it is usually fixed on the front edge of the upper board. The books were normally kept with their forages outwards, and on these edges the titles were written or emblazoned.

The Laurentian Library at Florence has a large number of chained books kept in beautifully carved shelves.

The Church of St. Wallberg in Zutphen has several chained books. There is a legend that the devil carried off so many of the holy books that something had to be done, so the chains were blessed in due form with holy water, since when the books have been safely preserved.

Plenty of examples of chained libraries are still left in England, particularly at Hereford Cathedral, the old treasure house at Wimborne Minster and All Saints' Church at Hereford; a complete list of them is given in Blades' "Books in Chains," published in London in 1892.

The inconvenience of chains must have been considerable, and no doubt careless readers often got into trouble about them. On a notice concerning the library at King's College, Cambridge, in 1683, readers are requested to replace the volumes "decently without entangling the chains."

About the middle of the eighteenth century the inconvenience of chains on books was fully realised, and from that time there has been a general tendency to their removal, except in cases where their retention is advisable for antiquarian reasons.

True horn books were used in England and America, but similar constructions also existed in other countries—chiefly France, Germany, Italy, and Holland—but without horn covering.

They were for children's use, and the alphabet and the Lord's Prayer are the commonest letterings upon them, always beginning with a cross, giving the first line the name of the "Christ cross" or "criss cross" row. The paper for true horn books is printed only on one side, and then laid down upon a flat piece of wood. Some unused eighteenth century horn book sheets are preserved in the Bagford fragments at the British Museum. Over the printed slip a piece of horn is put, kept in place by strips of brass fastened with nails having facetted tops, but it must be noted that after about 1820 the facetted tops were often replaced by flat heads.

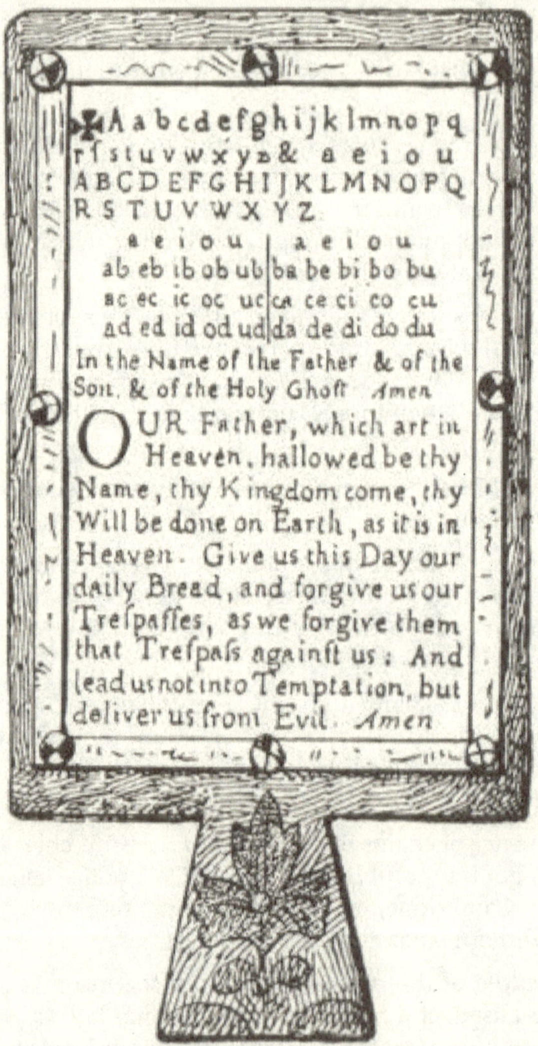

Fig. 85.—English seventeenth century horn book.

Like all books or objects which were originally cheap and common, horn books are now very rare, but they are so valuable that it is unluckily worth while to imitate them, and many fraudulent modern specimens are about. A horn book is, unfortunately, easy to copy, and it is sometimes a very difficult thing to say positively whether a given specimen is genuinely old or not. Modern frauds are often wrong in either the printing, the paper, the horn, or the nails, but they are often right as to the wood, which is easily made to have every proper appearance of age by means of soaking in water, rubbing with sand, staining by ammonia, and so on. Collectors should, if possible, get a properly authenticated history with every specimen offered to them.

Small plaques for teaching the alphabet seem to have existed before the invention of printing, but in printed form they were most used towards the end of the sixteenth century until the nineteenth, when their character altered, the wooden frame and its horn covering disappeared, and a degenerate production in varnished cardboard, preserving the old form in some respects, took their place. These cards are often called battledores, but this name was an old one, and originally used for true horn books. The name battledore is probably derived from the batlet, which was used for beating clothes, the horn books somewhat resembling this in shape.

Although the general run of horn books are simple, there are many instances in which they have been decorated; a certain analogy thus exists between the diptychs and the horn books. Lord Egerton of Tatton has a beautiful sixteenth century example, the back of which is ornamented with silver filigree work, and horn books backed with Dutch silver, engraved, are sometimes found. These generally have a bird or a tulip engraved upon them.

Other ornamental examples are to be found in the Birmingham Museum and in private ownership. They are very decorative, and some of them have talc instead of horn in front.

In 1851 some curious stone moulds were found at Hartley Castle by Sir George Musgrave, and one of them was undoubtedly used for casting lead "horn" books, and similar moulds have been found in Germany; the English ones may have been made about the earlier half of the sixteenth century.

But more curious devices were found on the other side of the same piece of stone: these are undoubtedly the emblems of saints' days as shown on clog almanacks of the same period, so that the horn books may possibly have originated from the makers of cast leaden almanacks.

Horn books were also cut in ivory or bone, often with designs engraved on the back or on the handle. The lettering and devices were originally run in with heel-ball or some such material. They were also made of boxwood with letters burnt in, or engraved pewter, or gingerbread, and sometimes covered in paper with panel stamp impressions in blind or black ink.

Several of the later seventeenth and early eighteenth century horn books were covered with leather and stamped in blind, gold, silver, or, in Dutch examples, Dutch metal, which nearly always turns black, from panel stamps; sometimes the designs were arabesques or flowers, and at other times we find figures of saints or kings—St. George and the Dragon, mermaids, and the like—and several of Charles II. on horseback, the Duke of Cumberland, and other great people.

These same stamps are also often impressed on paper backs as well as on leather.

The late cardboard horn books either leave out the cross at the beginning or replace it by a meaningless X; they also often show additional alphabets with little wood-cut illustrations. At last the horn book form is quite lost, and at last we find folded pieces of cardboard with stamped or marbled backs, retaining only the alphabet to show that they are survivals.

WORKS TO CONSULT.

BLADES, W.—Books in Chains. *London*, 1892.

DAVENPORT, C.—English Embroidered Bookbindings. *London*, 1899.

DAVENPORT, C.—Book Edges. (Bibliographica.)

DAVENPORT, C.—Little Gidding. (Bibliographica.)

DAVENPORT, C.—Royal English Bookbindings. *London*, 1897.

LABARTE, J.—Hist. des Arts Industriels au Moyen Age. *Paris*, 1864-66.

LACROIX, P.—Le Moyen Age et la Renaissance. *Paris*, 1848-51.

LIBRI, COUNT G.—Monuments Inedits. *Londres*, 1862.

PRIDEAUX, S. T.—Historical Sketch of Bookbinding. *London*, 1893.

TUER, A.—History of the Horn Book. *London*, 1896.

WOOLNOUGH, C. W.—The Art of Marbling.

CHAPTER VII.

LEATHERS.

Vellum—Calf—Pig skin—Sheep skin—Goat skin—Seal skin, etc.

Prepared skins of animals have been the most generally used of all materials for covering bindings of manuscripts or printed books. Leather is tanned skin, and the hair is generally removed. Bindings that have the hair still left on the leather are usually of an elementary kind and are intended to be carried about in pockets. They are not common. Vellum (calf skin), and parchment (sheep skin), are not tanned, but are prepared with lime and are white. Not uncommonly, especially in Germany, other skins were so prepared. Pig skin, deer skin, goat skin, horse skin, and donkey skin were all "vellumised," and are all very strong and take excellent impressions in blind.

It is likely enough that vellum was used for the first covering of books, simply enclosing the sections, the ends of the bands drawn in, without boards. Such bindings are excellent for thin books, and they were successfully re-introduced in recent times by William Morris, always used with ties, as otherwise the vellum crinkles up.

"Vellum" bindings made now, unless specially ordered, are only ordinary bindings in boards covered with vellum. Vellum is strong, but has some disadvantages. Although gold looks beautiful upon vellum it is difficult to work, and title labels do not stick to it well. If kept near the light it turns to something very like egg-shell and chips off. This defect was known to librarians in past times, and they met it by keeping their vellum books backs inwards, the forages outwards. Many instances of this manner of keeping vellum books occur in the Bodleian Library at Oxford, and they generally have their old pressmarks, and sometimes titles, written across the top of the forage. Old vellum was cut thick, and seldom ornamented, and if kept dry in the dark it is an excellent material. The same peculiarities exist in the case of parchment, which is, however, a very inferior skin, thinner, weaker, and not so good looking. Parchment is frequently described, and used, as vellum, and few purchasers know the difference; but the market value of parchment is less than half that of vellum. Vellum is particularly well suited for bindings kept in large towns, as dust does not stick to it, and it is easily cleaned. In time it assumes a creamy colour that is delightful. From the late sixteenth century until now, vellum stained green has been commonly used in England.

White vellumised leather, probably deer skin, has always been much liked in England from the time of Henry VIII., many of whose books were bound in this material: among them a copy of Elyot's "Image of Governance," printed in London in 1541, which is one of the first books with gold tooling upon it done in this country. Several books were bound in the same thick white leather for the other Tudor sovereigns, as well as for some of their richer subjects, but in the seventeenth century limp vellum once more asserted its sway and became very popular in England for highly valued books. The brilliancy of the gilding upon some of these bindings is quite wonderful; it is certainly doubtful if any modern finishers could equal the technical beauty of the work. Then in the eighteenth century, vellum, though still much esteemed, only took its place as a covering for boards, and once more, in the nineteenth century, Morris restored it to its proper use as a limp binding.

In 1785, James Edwards of Halifax patented a way of rendering vellum transparent, so that paintings underneath it showed through, and he used it with much success. The process has been revived of late years in England.

The Dutch binders have always liked vellum, but it is used with boards and never limp. Dutch vellum bindings are usually coloured, not well done, but at a distance they look decorative, and were certainly very popular. They often have clasps and painted edges.

A few bindings have been made in England, France, and Holland, covered with pierced vellum, showing coloured silk underneath. They are not very satisfactory and soon get out of order.

After vellum comes calf, the outer skin of the same animal, tanned. Calf is a good second, and I think altogether, up to about the end of the eighteenth century, that it has been more used than any other leather. The main difference between old calf and modern calf is that the old leather was properly tanned with oak bark or sumach, and cut thick, whereas modern calf used for binding is abominably tanned, quickly and disastrously, and cut thin. There is no better leather than old calf, and it was used universally; England, France, Germany, and Italy all liked it; it was delightful to decorate, either in blind or gilt, and it mellowed with age to a rich mahogany brown. Italian and sixteenth century English binders stained their fillets black, and several of these calf bindings, richly gilded, and with black fillets, are quite splendid, in perfect taste.

The surface of calf is smooth, and it is very sensitive to all sorts of stains.

Calf is seen at its best when it is used to take impressions from panel stamps, but its beautiful surface and sensitiveness to stains of all kinds has made it a favourite ground for all sorts of fancy markings, most of which, however charming they may be at first, end by destroying the leather.

Russia leather is calf prepared with willow bark and scented with birch oil. It is a modern leather, and lasts badly, and is generally diced,—that is to say, covered all over with diagonal rulings. It was a favourite leather of Roger Payne's. It is said that a book bound in Russia leather will last better if much used, and no doubt this is true, not only of Russia but of any other leather. As a rule leather bindings in libraries are starved; they get dry, and readily absorb animal oil from the human hand. The truth of this may be found in the fact that numbers of dictionaries and books of reference were preferentially bound in Russia leather some thirty or forty years ago, and whereas unused books bound at the same time in the same way now show rotting leather, the reference books which have been continually used are quite sound and supple.

Cow hide is like a magnified calf leather, and shows a slightly pitted surface. It is not often used, but is of much value for very large books that are worth full binding, as one piece of hide could be cut large enough, for instance, to full-bind the *Skibbereen Eagle*, one of the largest Irish newspapers. It would take three or four of the largest goat skins to do this, and it is always advisable to avoid joins, wherever possible, in a binding. But there is one drawback to the use of hide for binding: it is practically impossible to cut it smooth; however skilfully it may be pared, when it gets on the book it is always ridgy. This is, of course, not very important, but it militates against the use of hide except when absolutely necessary. For the rest, hide takes colour well, and it is a very handsome leather, and when it is finished simply with very broad gold fillets it is very ornamental.

Pig skin is perhaps the most familiar of all bookbinding leathers to the outside world, because saddles are made of it. It is a thick, rich leather, and, so to speak, full of life. It is not suitable for small books, but very good for large ones, and has been used in England off and on for a long time, but never very much. Charles Lewis executed some fine examples of his larger bindings in pig skin, but I think he never cared much for it.

Pig skin responds admirably to treatment with lime, the same method of preparation as used for vellum; and this white "vellumised" pig skin has always been the most favoured material for the covering of fine German books of the fifteenth, sixteenth, and seventeenth centuries. Many of these bindings are perfect in their way, covered all over with delicate roll stamps showing marvellous definition and clearness on the hard white surface.

Fine though all their impressions are, it cannot be denied that they are difficult to see; the impressions are shallow, and indeed the designs can often be more easily made out by help of a rubbing with heelball on soft white paper than by examining the binding itself.

Pig skin can be recognised by its smooth hard surface, strongly pitted with bristle holes. It is closely imitated in inferior leather, bristle holes and all, and when such imitation is actually on a book it is very difficult to detect, but if in skin form it can easily be recognised. In real pig skin the bristle holes penetrate right through the leather, and show quite as much at the back as they do in the front, whereas in the imitation they show little, if at all, at the back. Also the back of real pig skin is of very firm, close texture, but the imitation shows a more or less woolly or loose grained back, as it is generally made of sheep skin. French binders have never favoured pig skin much—it is not dainty enough for them.

Sheep skin has always been a favourite leather for bookbinding, but it is not a fine leather and has never been used for first-rate binding. It has, however, been more worked up than anything else into imitations of fine leathers.

The imitation of fine leather in inferior sheep skin has been for a long time a very important industry, and it is one which is still with us. All fine leathers show a particular and well known grain on their surface, but the most largely imitated is that of goat skin or morocco.

In a well grained skin of morocco, the beautiful grain is strongly marked, whether it be "pinhole" or "straight"—so strongly marked indeed that a cast of it can well be made in plaster of paris. From such a cast a metal die can be made, and when this die is strongly pressed upon a prepared piece of sheep skin, which will take an impression extremely well, the result is that a surface is produced which is so exactly like a piece of morocco that even a leather expert may be, and often is, taken in by it. In course of time, however, the impression flattens out, and the fraud betrays itself.

When such a stamped sheep skin is new on a book, and finished with gold, no one would for a moment suspect its genuineness, but if in skin form, the back of the leather will at once betray it. Real morocco has a hard close grain, but the back of the imitation will show a loose soft texture. Other leathers are imitated in the same way: pig skin, lizard skin, and others; and although there has been, and still is, much of such imitation used in the matter of bookbindings, there is still more of it used in the furniture trade.

But putting aside these base uses of sheep skin, it has a very fair record to show on its own unaided merits. Many early Italian bindings, good ones, were made in sheep skin; certainly it has not lasted well, but no doubt when new it was pleasing enough. In England, many of the early fifteenth century panel stamp bindings were made in sheep skin, not quite satisfactory now, but also probably well enough when new.

It is impossible to say much in favour of modern roan, the trade name for sheep skin, which has suffered badly at the hands of the tanner and the dyer; also probably the binders have not been without fault, as in order to get the leather flexible for joints and bands they have acquired a pernicious habit of paring it too thin, and another, equally hurtful, of unduly pulling and stretching it so that the fibres, or what is left of them, get strained and broken.

Skiver is part of a split sheep skin, the surface of which is altogether artificial. It is much used for cheap pamphlet bindings and looks well for the moment, but is not so strong as good paper. It is wonderful how cleverly the "paste grain" or artificial surface of skiver is made; it deceives most people easily. The remaining part of a split sheep skin is prepared quite differently and is made into "chamois" leather. Although this is not used for actual bindings, it is often enough made into linings for loose covers of fine books. It does well for this purpose, but must be kept in a very dry place as it has a certain affinity for damp.

The finest of all leathers for binding is goat skin, morocco as we now call it, from the reputed land of its origin. "Levant morocco" is still the name of the finest skins. Goats, however, have of course been common enough all over the world for ages, and so we find very ancient bindings in goat skin, quite possibly the most ancient, although I rather incline to vellum in this connection.

Many of the English twelfth to fourteenth century blind tooled bindings are in goat skin, tanned brown, most likely with oak bark, and from that period until now it has always been used here, at some periods more than others.

Goat skin always shows small hair dots in groups all over its surface; it is not quite smooth like calf, and also it shows certain structural striations. In early goat bindings both these marks show clearly, and until the time of Roger Payne in the eighteenth century, the leather was left in its natural state so far as surface marks went.

Italian bookbinders at an early date saw the beauty of natural sunk lines on goat skin, and accentuated them by rubbing in gold leaf. On such bindings the markings on the leather show as fine gold lines; it is a pretty idea, and can often be found on sixteenth century bindings, especially on those that were made for Tommaso Maioli.

French morocco bindings are frequently stained with colour, particularly those which were made about the time of Henri II. in the sixteenth century. The stain is usually put on the fillets or arabesques surrounding a central oval, in which is often a painted coat-of-arms. But as a rule such coloured bindings are in calf, which takes stain more easily than morocco.

Goat leather has never been so much liked by German binders as calf or pig skin. This is partly due to the fact that German bindings are as a rule ornamented with blind tooling, and goat skin is never satisfactory when treated in this way: its grain is against it; but for gold tooling, which has been brought to its greatest perfection by Italian, French and English binders, there is nothing that gives so fine a result as goat leather.

Roger Payne saw and liked the natural grain of goat skin, or, as we may now call it, morocco. But he found that in many cases he could get a better impression from his very delicately cut stamps in Russia leather. Here, however, he was restricted to one colour, and his favourite colour, a neutral green, could only be procured in morocco. So he ironed the morocco to flatten its natural hills and dales, and produced something like what is now called "crushed" morocco. Payne's smooth morocco is, however, not quite our modern "crushed"; it is smoother, because now we "grain" our leather strongly before crushing it, whereas Payne ironed his without first increasing its natural grain by artificial means. Morocco is often badly injured by the ironing being done with irons that are too hot.

But Payne went a step farther. No doubt he experimented much with morocco, and it is likely enough that before endeavouring to smoothen out his skins he wetted them thoroughly. If he wetted a fine skin of morocco overnight and left it alone, perhaps doubling it or rolling it up, he would have noticed next morning that the natural grain had become much intensified, due to a slight shrinkage of the leather, and showed as a particularly effective breaking up of the surface. Some such chance led him to make definite experiments with a view to exaggerating the natural grain of morocco, and he very soon found out that if a damped skin was well rolled in one direction it assumed permanently what is now known as a "straight" grain. That is to say, the surface of the leather is lined in the same sort of way as a ploughed field is, but not quite so regularly. The ridges and furrows all run in one direction. Several of Payne's bindings are bound in straight grain morocco, but judging from his own work, he never got any farther with his graining.

At a later time, I think towards the middle of the nineteenth century, it was found out that if the process of straight graining was carried out a second time at right angles to the first operation, the little straight furrows and ridges were broken up, and a surface was produced that consisted of a series of minute hillocks, like a field that has been harrowed, and this is known as a "pin-head" grain. Both these grainings improve the strength of the leather, as it contracts after the wetting and also the wear falls on the tops of the ridges or hillocks before it reaches the body of the leather.

French binders have always preferred smooth or crushed morocco for their bindings, as it is easier to gild upon. Morocco is sensitive to damp, and if affected it quickly betrays it by giving out the strong scent of goat which is normally quite absent.

Two new leathers have been recently put upon the market as rivals of morocco: one of these is seal skin and the other the skin of the sea-lion.

Seal skin is finished in the same way as morocco and looks very like it, but it is, I think, not so good. It is softer, more full of oil and has a peculiar, almost fishy, smell. The softness of seal leather makes it unfit for binding books that are likely to have much hard wear, but the oiliness is probably its worst fault, as books standing next to it are apt to be stained. But it is undoubtedly a good-looking and useful leather, and if it can be put upon the market at a less cost than morocco it is sure to have a considerable vogue. Sea-lion skin is only fit for use on big books; it is very strong and is curiously ridged in large ridges. It has the same oiliness that seal has, but not in so marked a degree.

There are, of course, several other leathers in which books have been bound as curiosities, and these are generally noted in some way; a book in the British Museum is lettered outside "Kangaroo," and manuscript notes are in others telling us in what strange materials they are covered. Fish skin, known as shagreen, has sometimes been used for bindings; it is very strong but inelastic, and soon goes at the joints. In the seventeenth century it was largely imitated in calf, stamped with a grain.

Perhaps the most curious leather in which any book can be bound is human skin. Such treasures are by no means unknown. It is said that a friend of Camille Flammarion the French writer, possessed beautiful shoulders, and that when she died she bequeathed her skin to him as he had always admired it. He had the skin tanned and used some of it for a binding of one of his own books, "Ciel et Terre." There are other examples in private ownership, but so far as public libraries are concerned the only instance I know of is now in the Carnavalet Library at Paris. It is a copy of the Constitution of 1793, and is bound in the skin of one of the revolutionaries who was killed at the time. The skin was tanned at Meudon. Human skin, undyed, looks like thick calf, and it is most difficult to get entirely rid of the hair.

It is to be regretted that of late years the desire for beautifully coloured leathers has induced the need for much treatment before the dyes, mostly aniline, could be properly applied. In the course of this treatment there has been an undue use of sulphuric acid, and the presence of this acid is fatal to the lasting qualities of any leather. Attention has, however, been drawn to the evil from authoritative sources, and now sound leathers can be obtained, and it is to be hoped that the public will second the endeavours of the committee appointed by the Society of Arts by always insisting on the use of sound and certified leather to bind their valuable books in.

BOOKS TO CONSULT.

SOCIETY OF ARTS.—Report of the Committee on Leather for Bookbinding. *London*, 1905.

LIBRARY ASSOCIATION.—Leather for Libraries. *London*, 1905.

CHAPTER VIII.
THE ORNAMENTATION OF LEATHER BOOKBINDINGS WITHOUT GOLD.

Blind tooling and stamping—Panel stamps—Cut leather—Stained calf—Cut vellum—Transparent vellum.

The true binding of a book consists of the sewing of the sections on bands, and the covering of leather is really wanted to protect the threads on the outer surfaces of the raised bands.

But this is generally taken for granted, and now when we speak of the binding of a book we normally mean only the outside ornamentation. In short, the term has changed its meaning; so in the remainder of this chapter, when I speak of the "binding" of a book, it is to be understood as the generally accepted meaning: namely, those parts of the leather covering that are visible.

From an artistic and æsthetic point of view we are justified in considering only the final ornamentation of a book binding. We rightly presume that in all great bindings, and even in the case of most good bindings, the technical procedures have all been truly and properly carried out. It is safe to presume this in the case of all bindings made before the latter half of the nineteenth century, but I regret to say that it is not safe to say it of bindings made then and later. There has been much improper use made of false bands, false headbands, "sawn in" backs, bad leather, and scamped sewing of sections even in books costing upwards of a hundred pounds for their bindings.

The consideration of the ornamentation of leather bindings without the use of gold is of itself a large study, and one that has received much attention of late years. In the trade, ornamental outside work is called "finishing," as distinct from the previous work, which is known as the "forwarding." As a rule, now, these operations are not done by the same hands, but a finisher does the finishing only and makes it his speciality.

Patterns stamped on leather by means of punches or small dies are found in numbers of early instances on horse trappings, shoes and boots, and accoutrements of various sorts; and almost as soon as it was found out that skins of animals could be rendered soft so as to be wearable, it was also found out that they could be ornamented by patterns cut or impressed upon them.

Such patterns are made when the leather is damp and soft, and on drying they become hard and permanent. Many of the earlier impressions made on leather bindings are done by means of hard styles held in the hand and drawn along the leather. Beautiful Celtic interlacings done in this way are found in the ancient Irish "polaires" or book covers. Others are small ornamental stamps which have been impressed on the leather in the same way as we now make an ordinary seal.

One of the earliest instances of a leather binding with ornamental covers is on a Coptic MS. on papyrus, dating from about the eighth century, which has been originally stabbed, and the pattern is an interlacing one with ornamented fillets, between which are impressions from small cameo stamps. In time special tools were carefully cut in hard wood or metal for the avowed purpose of ornamenting leather bindings. The exact date at which this occurred it is impossible to say.

So far as Europe is concerned, the earliest known blind tooled bindings range from about the twelfth century onwards. Earlier books were either covered with the rich metal and jewelled mediæval work that I have already noticed, or else bound in vellum with ties and without ornamentation.

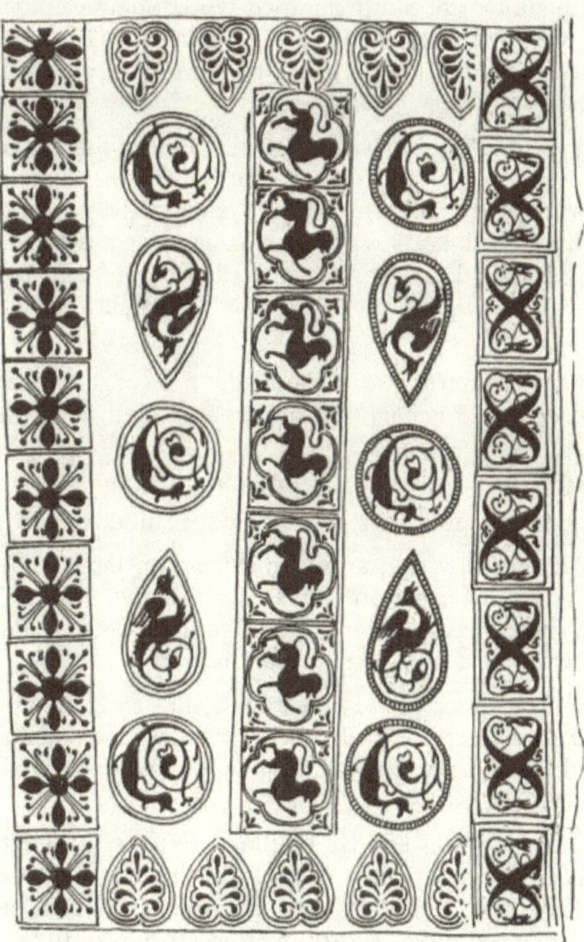

Fig. 86.—English blind tooled binding, 12th century. London.

In England the art of blind tooling reached its highest level from the twelfth to the fourteenth century, and, thanks to the researches of Mr. W. H. J. Weale, there is little doubt that the English excelled in this art. The Germans succeeded best after the English, but German work never approaches the English, either for excellence of general design or for delicacy and beauty of the small engraved stamps. The English work was on goat skin or calf, the German generally on pig skin.

The stamps used in blind tooling—that is to say, without gold—are cut in the same manner as a seal stone is, only that the cutting is much deeper, and in deep places needs no finishing. When this is pressed upon the soft, damp leather, the leather rises up of itself into the deep hollows cut in the stamp, and so a charming, natural, and apparently much studied relief is automatically given. Such stamps are called "cameo" stamps because of this relief.

The general typical arrangements used by England, Germany, and France in planning out the disposition of the stamps is a subject that is deserving of careful attention by any student of blind stamped work. Some valuable plans of these dispositions can be found in Mr. W. H. J. Weale's *Catalogue of Bookbindings and Rubbings of Bindings in the National Art Library, South Kensington*, and they are well worthy of study.

Roughly, it will be found that the most elaborate of these bindings have come from Durham, London, Winchester, or Oxford, that series of close perpendicular lines of small stamps are characteristic of French early stamped work, and that the marking out of the boards with large lozenges is a German plan. But these types must not be studied alone, as they travelled about freely; the character of the stamps themselves, as well as the leather used, must all receive careful consideration.

London bindings often show perpendicular lines of stamps, sometimes touching, sometimes separate; several of the stamps are round, and others drop-shaped.

The Winchester Domesday Book, now in the library of the Society of Antiquaries, is a beautiful and typical specimen of English twelfth century blind tooling. It is bound in deep brown goat skin, and each side is differently ornamented.

The upper board shows an arrangement of two large circles, largely made up by impressions of the common English drop-shaped stamps. These circles are flanked by two rows of rectangular stamps bearing monsters, and the corners are filled in with circular and drop-shaped stamps.

Durham bindings must be studied at Durham Cathedral, where Bishop Pudsey's books are kept. They are twelfth century work, and splendid examples. On some of these bindings occur interlacings of basket work designs, borrowed from the East.

One of the most curious English bindings in existence is known as St. Cuthbert's Gospels. Its history is of great interest. It is a copy of the Gospel of St. John, and is said to have been buried with St. Cuthbert at Lindisfarne in the seventh century. The saint's coffin was shortly afterwards moved to Durham. The tomb was opened in the reign of Henry I. in 1105, when the little copy of the Gospel was found in it, and removed and kept in the treasury at Durham.

Fig. 87.—English binding of St. Cuthbert's Gospels, in embossed leather.

It then passed through many hands, and at last found a home at Liège, whence one of the Jesuit Fathers brought it to Stonyhurst College, where it now is.

The binding is of thin lime wood covered with red leather, the upper board is ornamented with a nearly square central panel bearing a Celtic scroll in raised work. Above and below this are two rectangular panels ornamented with scroll-work impressed with a style and coloured by hand with blue and yellow paint. A narrow border is ornamented with a twisted line painted yellow. On the lower cover is a geometrical design drawn in lines and also coloured yellow.

It is not known what the date of this binding is, and it is likely enough that the extraordinary state of preservation in which it still is may be due either to very careful keeping, or else that the seventh century work has been carefully copied on one or other of the many occasions during which such copy could easily have been made.

Fig. 88.—English binding of the twelfth century, with bronze figure of Christ.

Mr. Gordon Duff inclines to about the tenth century, but I should imagine that the most likely time for such a copy to be made was when the tomb of St. Cuthbert was opened in 1105, and the book, then some four hundred years old, was removed. It is likely enough that the authorities of the Cathedral library treasury at Durham would have admired the binding, which was probably much out of condition, and had it carefully copied in new leather.

Even if it were made then, it would still be the earliest decorative English binding left, apart from blind tooled work, and it is undoubtedly a most decorative and effective example. But it is permissible to think and hope that at all events it preserves the colour and designs of the seventh century binding, which was the first cover of the old manuscript.

Another very early English binding, covering a Latin Psalter of the early twelfth century with interlinear Saxon version, is now kept in the British Museum among the Stowe collection.

It is bound in oaken boards nearly an inch thick, the central portion of which is hollowed into a rectangular depression. On the lower board is a bronze figure of our Lord in the attitude of the Crucifixion. The figure has been gilded, but most of the gold has now worn off. The corners have small bosses set in triangular pieces of thin metal, which are impressed with a design of a *fleur-de-lys* in outline within a circle. The boards are covered with brown leather, much worn and faded, probably deer skin, and the brass fastenings for a clasp still remain *in situ*.

The history of the book is as curious as the book itself; there are several manuscript notes in it, and also much has been written about it.

It appears to be the original book on which our sovereigns took their coronation oath, and it seems to have been so used from the coronation of Henry I. to that of Henry VII.

Powell in his *Repertory of Records* mentions this as a fact, and it was repeated by Thos. Madox, historiographer, and also by Thos. Astle, Keeper of the Records in the Tower of London, to whom it belonged, and it is believed to have been written and bound for the coronation of Henry I.

From the library of Thomas Astle the little book passed into the possession of the Marquis of Buckingham, and was kept at Stowe in a beautiful Gothic room built for a library. In June, 1849, the Stowe library changed hands and became the property of Lord Ashburnham, and in 1883 it was acquired by the Trustees of the British Museum.

So the coronation book is now the property of the nation, and in company with the greater part of the Stowe library, but the Irish MSS., some of them in beautiful bindings, went to Ireland, where they are now safely kept in the library of the Royal Irish Academy.

Caxton's styles of binding are not distinctively English in character. The reason for this is that in all probability he brought foreign stamps and styles with him when he returned from Bruges and set up in Westminster in 1477. So the few blind stamped bindings that appear to have issued from Caxton's workshop bear the diamond-shaped spaces characteristic of foreign work, filled with impressions for cameo stamps, often triangular. Wynkyn de Worde used the same stamps.

Fig. 89.—English blind tooled bindings. Caxton. (1491.)

White deer skin bindings were used much in England in the fifteenth century; they were unornamented, and usually had small clasps. A fine copy of the Book of St. Albans, in a contemporary binding of this kind, was recently sold by Mr. Quaritch.

A curious treatise in bookbinding, the earliest known, is in the Bibliothèque Nationale; but there are two treatises by John Bagford which may be of about the same date, early in the eighteenth century. These treatises have been published by the Bibliographical Society, and are full of interesting matter. Bagford mentions inscriptions on stone, "slate books," or diptychs, paste-boards, sewing, headbands, covers, bosses, clasps, horn books, and gives curious rules for collating, folding, and binding.

At Oxford fine blind tooled bindings were produced in considerable numbers. In the fifteenth century Theodoric Rood and Thomas Hunt did fine work, and in the seventeenth, Dominick Pinart and Edward Miles were especially prominent. The main characteristic of early Oxford bindings is the presence of small rectangular stamps closely arranged in rows.

Cambridge has also been notable among English towns for the production of fine blind tooled bindings. The main characteristic of these bindings may, perhaps, be considered to be the existence of rolls on which are variations of the Royal Tudor badges, rose, fleur-de-lys, portcullis, the castle of De Beaufort, and the pomegranate. Larger rolls have devices of monsters, and frequently the initials of the binders may be found.

In the sixteenth century the works of Garrett Godfrey, Nicholas Spierinck and John Siberch are, perhaps, most usually met with. They show the initials of their respective binders.

Fig. 90.—French blind stamped binding of the sixteenth century.
With figure of S. Barbara.

Fig. 91.—English blind stamped binding, with the arms of Henry VIII.

Blind tooled bindings of French origin are numerous enough, especially those impressed with panel stamps. The main characteristic of early work is the existence of perpendicular lines of blind tooling, but although this peculiarity is often-er found on French work than on any other, it is by no means unknown in bind-ings made by English and German workmen, so must not be taken as an absolute proof of French origin if unsupported by other evidence.

Late in the fifteenth century the panel stamp was invented in Holland, or the Netherlands, and it soon attained a great measure of popularity. It reached England in the early part of the sixteenth century, and although at first foreign dies were freely used here, in time our native binders made their own.

In France and Germany panel stamps were also popular, used on calf bind-ings, but I think that in Italy it never made much headway.

The Netherlands panel stamps often have the names of the binders upon them, Bollcaert, Bloc, and many more, and the same valuable information is also often found on French panel stamps of the sixteenth century.

The best known names are André Boule, Jean Moulin, R. Macé, and Denis Roce. All these are plentiful, and are often found in excellent condition. The English panel stamps do not bear names upon them, but they often have initials, but whether it is safe to interpret these is difficult to say. We generally consider that J. R. stands for John Reynes, I. N. for Jean Norins, R. L. for Richard Lant, G. G. for Garrett Godfrey, R. P. for Richard Pynson, and so on; but it is probable, anyhow, that although panel stamps of English design bearing these initials were used here, they were largely of foreign, probably Netherlandish, origin.

Fig. 92.—English sixteenth century panel stamp,
with the initials of Julian Notary.

In the early sixteenth century in England, heraldry was an important science, and began to show itself as a fertile source of ornamentation of bindings. Many of the panel stamps of the early Tudor period are heraldic. The most interesting of these stamps is one which is found in combination with several others; it seems to be a sort of backbone. The design consists of a large Tudor rose, partly enclosed by ribbon on which is the legend HEC ROSA VIRTUTIS DE CŒLO MISSA SERENO ETERNUM FLORENS REGIA SCEPTRA FERET.

Fig. 93.—English blind stamped binding, with the arms
of Queen Katherine of Arragon.

At the side are two angels and in the corners the arms of London and the Cross of St. George.

Then there are numbers of other stamps bearing in the centre the coat-of-arms of Henry VII. and Henry VIII. up to 1526, namely, France and England quarterly, with supporters, the red dragon of Cadwallader and the white greyhound of De Beaufort.

Belonging to the same school of design are fine panel stamps bearing the armorial devices of Anne Boleyn and Queen Katharine Parr.

The question as to whether these stamps are royal or not inevitably occurs to any student, but as with one or two exceptions they carry with them extraneous ornament, such as the sun and moon, and arms of London, I think that any such stamp cannot have been royal, but it is possible enough that when the royal arms alone are found the stamp may have been originally cut for royalty. Such stamps as these are very strong and are not likely to have ever been worn out—indeed, it is curious that instances of unauthorised use of royal stamps is not commoner than it is.

One of the most curious of these panel stamps, not armorial, is one which bears upon it the device of John Reynes. It shows a fancy coat-of-arms on which are the emblems of the Passion, with two unicorns as supporters, a royal helmet, above which are scourges, &c., and a crowing cock, and below on a ribbon the words "Arma redemptoris mundi." One cannot forget here that Dame Juliana Berners, in the Boke of Cote Armour, declares the Christ was a gentleman of coat armour by right of his mother Mary.

The English panel stamps, as well as rolls, of the early Tudor period often bear the Tudor badges of double or Tudor rose, the fleur-de-lys, and the portcullis of the De Beauforts. These badges are usually crowned.

Panel stamps were cut on latten, a metal alloy resembling brass. The thin engraved plate was fixed on a wooden block by means of two pegs, and the impression was made on the leather either by the use of a hammer or by means of weights, very likely by a combination of both these, methods.

After a time the pegs worked loose, and very frequently panel stamps are found in which the impression from these loosened pegs can be seen.

Many German calf bindings of the fourteenth, fifteenth, and sixteenth centuries are beautifully ornamented with cut work. The outlines of the designs are cut with a sharp small knife held slantingly, and afterwards worked into shape with blunted tools. The designs upon these bindings are often very fine, and the workmanship is most skilled and effective. The earliest example I know of is elaborately ornamented on the upper board with a groundwork of floral scrolls, and has in the centre the Austrian coat-of-arms supported on an eagle, which is stained black. On a scroll above the eagle are the words "Fridericus rex, etc., 1451" and below it in a long panel the letters "A E I O U," standing for the proud motto "Austria est imperare orbi universo." Along the lower edge is cut the name of the binder, "Petrus Ligator."

**Fig. 94.—English blind stamped binding, with arms of Christ.
Bound by John Reynes, c. 1530.**

Hunting scenes and scenes of religious life are usually found on these early German cut leather bindings, now and then, as in the case of the splendid sixteenth century copy of Ranierus de Pisa's *Pantheologia*, now in the British Museum, showing a monk at his desk; the borders are ornamented with small stamps. Cut leather bindings are done with consummate skill, and must always have been very costly, so we find that they were, and are, very cleverly imitated by skilfully cut stamps. An example of this is so well done that it has over and over again been described as hand work, but in fact it is only a stamp. German leather workers are still pre-eminent in this small cut manner. At the St. Louis Exhibition of 1904, in the German section there were several examples of cut leather work done in exactly the same way as the fifteenth century work—and quite as good. It is not only used for book bindings but also to cover boxes and small articles, but as we have noted in the case of earlier work, many modern apparently hand-cut German leathers are really only impressions from large panel stamps.

Fig. 95.—English blind stamped binding. Pynson, 1499.

Fig. 96.—German cut leather binding,
made for the Emperor Frederick of Austria. Dated 1451.

Fig. 97.—English blind stamped binding, with the arms of Henry VIII.

Notable among German bindings are those made by John Richenbach, of Gyslingen, who lettered and dated many of his fine volumes. The dates run from 1467 onwards. There is one fine example in the British Museum; it is like all the rest, in pig skin, and stamped in blind, a little transparent colour being put over many of the stamps. Round the outer borders of the boards runs the inscription in large black letters:

ILLIGATA PER ME IO. RICHENBACH CAPELLANU
IN GYSLINGEN, 1475.

All Richenbach's bindings are still thoroughly strong and good, and the small touch of colour upon them redeems them from the monotony of colour which is so marked in the later German bindings in white pig skin.

Fig. 98.—German binding, by J. Richenbach. Dated 1475.

German blind tooled bindings are very numerous, as the art was always much liked by German binders, and whereas both in England and in France blind tooling and stamping quickly gave way before the more beautiful and popular art of gold tooling, in Germany the quieter blind work has retained its supremacy. German binders never took kindly to gold tooling, and when they had to do it they generally used bad metal. Most early German gold tooled work is now badly discoloured for this reason.

**Fig. 99.—German stamped leather binding with portrait
of Charles V. Dated 1570.**

German bindings in calf are usually designed with a central panel crossed by diagonals at considerable intervals, and in the diamonds thus formed are impressions of various stamps. On white pig skin, however, are to be found the most characteristic of the German blind tooled works. We find large books elaborately ornamented with impressions of finely cut "cameo" rolls, and having a centre panel stamp showing the portrait of some notable person, or a coat-of-arms. The rolls are worthy of much attention, as they are very carefully designed and beautifully cut. They show an infinite variety of designs, and may be roughly divided into two classes, namely, those showing human figures, busts in profile, and those only bearing floral or arabesque designs. Among the former there is a long series of allegorical figures, all with their respective emblems, and often lettered and dated. There are Faith, Hope and Charity; Sweetness, Prudence, Justice; figures of the Evangelists, Christ, David, St. Paul, Lucretia, and heads of the reformers, Luther, Melancthon and Hus particularly.

Some of the German panel stamps are very large, also numerous and finely cut. There are splendidly executed stamps of Charles V. and other distinguished personages, emperors and grand dukes, Rudolf and many others, and others of Luther and Melancthon. Some of these are set in an arabesque framing with a space left in the middle for an insertion. These are found impressed on calf and on pig skin, and the dies of many of them are most beautifully cut.

Several of the later calf bindings, done in the eighteenth and nineteenth century, show an infinite variety of marblings, sprinklings and "tree" patternings, done with one or other of the most appropriate chemicals—potash, soda, oxalic acid—run on when the leather is wet. But one and all of these rot away the surface wherever they touch it, and many of these books can now be found from which the original dyed spots have all entirely disappeared, leaving, however, a little eaten-out depression in every case.

James Edwards, of Halifax, invented a style of ornamenting calf by means of ordinary book stamps loaded with acid. The result is not unpleasing, and such books are known as "Etruscan," because many of the designs are of classical feeling—little urns, the Greek fret and the like. But Edwards' little acid burnt designs are only used as accessories; there is plenty of gold work and ordinary blind work upon them as well.

John Whitaker, another eighteenth century binder, went a step further, and drew designs upon his calf bindings with pen or brush. Some of these are very effective, but as a rule they are now showing the effects of time, the original darkest places, where the acid has been most freely applied, suffering first, and showing the pale calf underneath. But a fine specimen of Whitaker's work is much to be prized. He also used the "Etruscan" style. He had many imitators, but whereas Whitaker's bindings are generally ornamented with figure drawings, the imitators as a rule preferred easier subjects—ruins or landscapes.

Calf with the rough side outwards, like brown velvet, was used in England from the seventeenth to the nineteenth century, sometimes tooled in blind and sometimes in gold.

Vellum was used at Little Gidding. One such book is covered in vellum painted orange colour and overlaid with openwork designs cut in white vellum. It is a harmony of the Gospels. The centre design is circular, and the corners have quarter circles. They are all helped with a little gold tooling.

In the sixteenth and seventeenth centuries several small French and Dutch books were prettily ornamented with vellum cut in openwork patterns. Underneath the open places bits of coloured silk are laid. They are dainty but not very successful, as small edges and points of the vellum are apt to curl up and catch.

James Edwards, of Halifax, invented a curious way of making vellum transparent, and patented it in 1785. The vellum had to be soaked in pearlash and subjected to various processes, pressure among them, and cut very thin indeed, so as to be more like goldbeater's skin than anything else. Then the books were covered with fine white paper and painted, generally in monotone, but sometimes in colour, and over this painting the transparent vellum was skilfully fixed. The result is that, except when the thin vellum is cracked or seen through, the painting underneath is as fresh as ever it was; but it is to be presumed that there is not much wearing strength in Edwards' vellum, chiefly because of its extreme thinness. But as a rule any fine examples of his work, especially as they look dainty and precious, have always been well kept and highly valued, and are in good and clean condition. Some modern binders have essayed Edwards' plan with a certain measure of success.

Impressions of designs in low relief were made on thin leather bindings by means of engraved cylinders in the earlier half of the nineteenth century. They were chiefly used in the small and beautifully illustrated periodicals which were so popular in England—*The Age, Friendship's Offering*, and many more—issued during the earlier half of the nineteenth century and a little after it. Charming designs in cameo are often found in these cases, on paste-boards covered with thin leather, but they are nearly always rubbed badly in projecting places. Some of the best of these designs are by Remnant and Edmonds, Smith Elder & Co., and De La Rue & Co.

BOOKS TO CONSULT.

BAGFORD's Notes on Bookbinding. (Bibliographical Soc. Proceedings, Nov. 16, 1903.)

BICKELL, L.—Buchereinbände des XV. bis, XVIII. Jahrhunderts aus hessischen Bibliotheken. *Leipzig*, 1892.

BOUCHOT, H.—Les reluires d'Art à la Bibliothèque Nationale. *Paris*, 1888.

DAVENPORT, CYRIL.—Cantor Lectures on Decorative Bookbinding. *London*, 1898.

DAVENPORT, CYRIL.—Early London Bookbindings. *London*. (*The Queen*, 1891.)

DUFF, E. G.—Early Stamped Bindings. (Prideaux, S. T.) *London*, 1893.

GIBSON, S.—Early Oxford Bindings. *London*, 1903.

Gibson, S.—Some Notable Bodleian Bindings. *Oxford*, 1901-4.

Gray, G. J.—The Earlier Cambridge Bookbinders. *London*, 1904.

Gray, G. J.—A Note upon Early Cambridge Binders of the Sixteenth Century. *Cambridge*, 1900.

Grolier Club, New York.—Catalogue of Decorated Early English Bookbindings exhibited ... 1899. *New York*, 1899.

Lindsay, J. L. (*Earl of Crawford*).—Early Bindings Exhibited at the Society of Antiquaries. *London*, 1886.

Weale, W. H. J.—Catalogue of Bookbindings ... in the National Art Library, South Kensington. *London*, 1894.

CHAPTER IX.
THE ORNAMENTATION OF LEATHER BOOKBINDINGS WITH GOLD.

Gold tooling in leather introduced from the East to Venice—Early Italian gold tooled work—The spread of gold tooling in Europe—Modern work—Gold tooling in leather—Early Venetian gold tooled bindings—The work of Thos. Berthelet, John Day, John Gibson, Mary Collet, Samuel Mearne, Suckerman, Eliot and Chapman, Roger Payne, Richard Wier, Charles Hering, Kalthœber, Staggemeier, Walther, Charles Lewis, T. J. Cobden Sanderson, Sir Edw. Sullivan, Douglas Cockerell, E. M. MacColl, S. Prideaux, Adams, Etienne Roffet, Geoffrey Tory, Nicholas and Clovis Eve, Le Gascon, Florimond Badier, Macé Ruette, L. A. Boyet, Padeloup le Jeune, J. Le Monnier, Derome le Jeune, Capé, Duru, Thouvenin, Bauzonnet, Trautz, Lortic.

The art of gold tooling on leather appears to have been known in Eastern countries before it was known in the West. There are signs of it in Saracenic work of the early fifteenth century, but it cannot be quite certain whether much of this work was not simply painted with gold. If a blind line is carefully painted with gold shell and then burnished with a fine agate, a gilded line can be made that looks nearly as well as a properly gold tooled line. No doubt a considerable proportion of early gold tooling was done in this way, and some of it was not even burnished.

Some early Venetian bindings show gold spaces gilded with gold leaf in a very effective way, and in the Bodleian some English panel stamps of the early sixteenth century are gilded all over.

There is little doubt that gold tooling, done as it is now, was known to the Venetians towards the end of the fifteenth century. It is a curious art, and depends for its wonderful strength upon the fact that albumen hardens with heat. The method used is simple: a stamp is impressed in blind on the leather, and then the impression is painted over with glaire of egg—albumen. When the albumen is dry it is again painted over with palm oil or cocoa-nut oil, and on this a piece of gold leaf is laid. The stamp is now heated, and when it is of the proper temperature it is very carefully reimpressed in exactly the same place as at first.

Fig. 100.—Italian gold tooled binding, 1514.

The heat of the stamp congeals the albumen under the gold, and the now gilded impression is likely enough to be the strongest part of the leather. I have often found old leather bindings badly worn away, but the gold tooled work and lettering still remaining in places. Thus, instead of being *impressed*, as it originally was, it is all in *relief*, because the albumen has soaked into the leather a little and then been hardened, so that instead of gilded hollows we find little mountains with golden tops.

But to counterbalance this possible advantage, the albumen presents a weak point. On an old gold tooled binding it is not uncommon to find that a golden curve is partly gone; half of it perhaps shows no longer as a thin gold line, but only as a shallow trench, hollowed out of the leather. The meaning of this is that the albumen provides a nourishing meal for some small grub, which, once it gets the trail, will follow it, if not disturbed half over the book, and with wonderful accuracy will eat away gold, albumen, and a little leather, following curves, leaves, and letterings with close fidelity.

This particular damage is most liable to occur in instances where books are laid down in show cases on cloth or velvet and not often moved. The soft groundwork allows the grub more freedom than if the book is standing up closely packed with others on a shelf.

The small gilt roundels found on early Persian and Arabic bindings as well as on early Venetian work, were set with some sort of gesso under the gold.

The trade of Venice with the East brought these matters of ornamented leather to the notice of Venetian bookbinders, and these, men of consummate taste, at once saw the possibilities of the new art. Indeed, the Italian gold tooled bindings of the late fourteenth century are the finest that have ever yet been made, even though many of them are quite Oriental in feeling and others very strongly so. But the Venetians soon crept away from the Eastern trammels and evolved beautiful styles of their own. One of the first of these styles was the careful mingling of blind tooled lines with gilded lines; another was the use of small gilded roundels—themselves an Oriental idea—in connection with blind tooling and blind tooling coloured by hand.

Fig. 101.—Cameo stamp of Apollo and Pegasus found on binding that belonged to D. Canevari. Italian, sixteenth century.

Then at an early date the Italians hit upon the effective use of so-called "cameo" stamps. These were sometimes cut on a flat piece of metal, as the "Canevari" stamps are, and sometimes on a bossed piece of metal, as the Alexander and Cæsar are. When on the binding these stamps show as a depression with the design in relief within it.

Many of the smaller stamps of this period are worthy of notice. There is the "Arabic" knot, used on Aldine binding and derived from an Oriental original from basket work, as many of the early stamps are, the Florentine leaf and the Aldine dolphin.

Fig. 102.—Italian gold tooled binding made for Jean Grolier.

Then there is no doubt that many of the finest of the bindings made for Jean Grolier were Italian. Who designed them and who bound them we do not know, but among the earlier examples there is no doubt that splendid work can be found. They may have been done in the workshop of Aldus Manutius, but it rather seems that the designs were made by one man, and I think it is not unlikely that Grolier himself may have always given the general idea of the decoration he wanted.

The later bindings made for Grolier are curiously inferior, and sometimes in calf. The earlier and finer bindings are in morocco, which is sometimes marbled. The words "Grolierii et Amicorum" are always put upon such bindings as were made for him, and the legend "Portio mea domine sit in terra viventium" also generally appears in the centre of one or other of the boards.

Fig. 103.—Italian gold tooled binding made for Jean Grolier, 1532.

Whenever Grolier acquired a book which was already very finely bound he added his autograph either on the flyleaf at the beginning or at the end. Grolier was the first collector to have his books bound in a particular way for himself.

"Grolier" bindings have been very freely imitated, especially by a native of Bologna, who worked a good deal for Count Guglielmo Libri, a great collector, and unfortunately the style lends itself well to imitation. A fraudulent finisher looks out for an old Italian book of the right date, bound in plain leather. Then he copies parts from one or other of the many Groliers which can be seen and studied by any Londoner or Parisian for the asking, and if he is fairly clever at his trade it will take a very skilled expert to detect the fraud. Many such imitations are about, and every day they become more like genuine examples.

Fig. 104.—English gold tooled binding by Thos. Berthelet. Made for Henry VIII.

The styles of binding that have been most largely and successfully imitated are those made for Jean Grolier, Henri II. and of his period, and the so-called "Canevari" bindings.

Fig. 105.—English binding by Thos. Berthelet, 1552. Made for Edward VI.

From Italy the art of gold tooling rapidly spread through Europe, and took hold particularly in England and France. There is no doubt that an Italian gilder came to England and taught Thomas Berthelet, binder and printer to Henry VIII. Not only are numbers of Berthelet's stamps of distinctly Italian character, but in many of his lists of books he describes particular examples as being bound "after the Italian fascion." But Berthelet quickly enough evolved a style of his own. It appears to me that English binders have from the time of Berthelet until now succeeded better than those of any other nation in the ornamentation of large books. In small books the palm must be given to Italian and French binders, but large books have always puzzled the best of these, and even Le Gascon has not been successful with them.

Many of the large books bound by Thomas Berthelet are as fine as any such books can be. His best work was, naturally enough, done for royalty, but he set the fashion for smaller binders, and although there is a want of minute finish and technical accuracy in everything he did, Berthelet's fine work will always give him a place in the first rank of bookbinders of this or any other country.

Fig. 106.—English inlaid and gold tooled binding by John Day.
Made for Queen Elizabeth.

**Fig. 107.—Italian inlaid and gold tooled binding in Oriental style.
Made for Queen Elizabeth.**

After Berthelet's time gold tooling became general in England, but the binders who used it are anonymous. There are some fine calf bindings with inlays of white leather which were made in the reign of Queen Elizabeth, on which appear the initials I. D. P., perhaps "John Day Pegit," and which are credited to John Day, but it is by no means certain that they were done by that eminent printer. The style of leather bindings of Elizabeth's reign departed finally from that of Berthelet, and more variety is found than at any other period. The Oriental fashion of double boards was re-introduced, the centre panels being filled with delicate paintings, portraits or coat-of-arms, and the remainder of the boards variously ornamented with inlays of white leather, toolings in gold and silver, and impressions from stamps cut in arabesques. Some of these bindings are coloured, that is to say, the arabesques, curves or flowers are painted by hand with some kind of enamel paint. The main source of such coloured bindings was Lyons, from which centre numbers of them were issued, but the fashion was one which appealed to the English liking for colour, and many fine examples, often heraldic, were made here. In royal bindings at all times heraldry has played an important part, but from the middle of the sixteenth century onwards it plays an equally important part on bindings made for ordinary armigerous people.

Letterings often appear on the sides of bindings of the Tudor period, mottoes, initials and names. Towards the end of the sixteenth century a few bindings are found on which are semis of triple dots. This is the beginning of the style which reached its ultimate form in the next century. Also small triangular corner stamps occur now and then. These also developed and eventually became one of the most characteristic marks of Jacobean bindings.

When James VI. of Scotland came here as our James I. he may have brought with him John Gibson, who was his binder in Scotland. Lists of books bound by this binder still exist, but no book or binding mentioned by him has so far been identified. But there are some remarkable books among those which were certainly bound for James I. which are not like the general type of his bindings, and it is likely enough that these may be Gibson's work. The style is a very fine one, and the workmanship strong and good, but not, in my opinion, correct enough to have been done by a foreign binder. The same binder did some of the re-binding for Henry Prince of Wales, and one of its characteristics is a dotted fillet of double lines.

Fig. 108.—The book stamp of Robert Dudley, Earl of Leicester.

Fig. 109.—The book stamp of Lord Burleigh.

It is probable that many of the richer bindings of the early seventeenth century were the work of John and Abraham Bateman, the king's printers and binders, but, in spite of lists, this is again only speculation. There is no doubt that about this time many bindings were made which would now be called trade bindings as apart from art bindings. Trade bindings often enough follow art bindings at a respectable distance, and they are rarely made on original lines.

Fig. 110.—English binding by Thos. Berthelet, 1537, with the title on the sides.

Fig. 111.—English Jacobean corner stamp.

Following the lead given by some of the later Elizabethan bindings, we find from about 1603 to 1625 a considerable output of very showy bindings, with elaborate semis or powderings of small stamps all over the groundwork, very large and over-elaborated corner stamps and centres of arabesque or heraldic motives.

Students of English royal bindings must note that with the coming of James I. to the English throne, a great change was made in the English coat-of-arms. The coat which had been used from the time of Edward III., namely, France and England quarterly, was now used as a quartering only, and shows in the first and fourth quarters. In the second quarter we find the ancient coat of Scotland, or, a lion rampant within a double tressure flory counterflory gu., and in the third quarter comes the coat of Ireland, az., the harp of Apollo Grian, stringed ar, *or.*, given, it is supposed, by Henry VIII. as a mark of admiration for the musical excellence of the Irish.

Fig. 112.—English gold-tooled binding made for James I.

Also the late Tudor supporters of the lion and dragon give place to the familiar lion and unicorn. The unicorn is one of the ancient supporters of the Scottish coat. It is interesting to note in passing that the present official coat of Scotland is, first and fourth Scotland, second England, and third Ireland, with two unicorns as supporters. It appears on Scottish official bindings. The interpretation of this is of course that England and Ireland are appanages of Scotland.

But even if it is now correct to dissociate the arms of England and Scotland, we must not forget the heraldic marriage between the two countries which took place in 1706, on which auspicious occasion the two coats were impaled as one. That is to say, they were treated in the same way as the coats of married people.

Fig. 113.—English inlaid and gold tooled binding made by Mary Collet at Little Gidding.

The semis, with large corners, is a manner which has lasted a long time, but it is not a great style; it is, however, one which has been largely followed in the case of trade bindings. In this manner a very rich and brilliant effect can be produced with a minimum of real design and of technical skill. The centres of such bindings, if not simply coats-of-arms, are always of oval outline, but at Little Gidding the irregular Jacobean corners and oval centres turned into circular centres and quarter-circle corners. The gold tooled leather bindings made at Little Gidding followed closely in detail those made by Thomas and John Buck, the Cambridge University printers, but in the main the bindings made by Mary Collet and her assistants were original. In the matter of semis also the Little Gidding bindings show a pleasant departure from the quite regular arrangements aimed at by Jacobean binders.

After 1625 the series and corners tended gradually to fall into abeyance, and although they did not altogether disappear, they were each modified. Corner pieces became smaller in proportion, and the semis more artistically irregular.

Towards the end of the reign of Charles I. some unknown binder, probably Samuel Mearne, had the hardihood for the first time to bind royal books without any ornamentation on the boards except a coat-of-arms. The red leather, goat skin, used on these bindings is of extremely fine colour and quality. Simplicity in ornamentation of bookbindings is usually accompanied by fine leather, and at no time has this been more noticeable than in the case of Mearne's simpler work.

Fig. 114.—Book stamp of the English Commonwealth.

The political troubles of the later half of the seventeenth century may of themselves have tended to incline bookbinders to simplify their work, and so also may the Puritan spirit of the time. State bindings of the time are studiously simple, and bear upon them a device with shields, showing the English cross of St. George and the harp of Ireland side by side, impressed upon black leather.

But there were other very decorative small bindings being produced in considerable numbers about this period. Whether these also owed their existence to Samuel Mearne is still uncertain, but he was, I expect, a moving spirit in the matter of fine bookbindings from the end of the reign of Charles I. to the end of the reign of Charles II. The little books I allude to were made during the latter half of the seventeenth century and are always bound in black morocco. They have inlays of red, yellow, and white leather upon them and some very well designed gold tooling. Many of the designs are in detail similar to those which were certainly used at a later time by Samuel Mearne. John Bagford, in a curious account of book binding written early in the eighteenth century, mentions a workman named Suckerman, who was "one of the best workmen that ever took tool in hand, and commonly worked for Mr. Merne the Binder to King Charles the 2."

It is quite possible that much of the finest English work of this period was done by this man, but I expect he was only a workman, and executed the designs made out for him by a skilled designer—possibly enough Mearne himself.

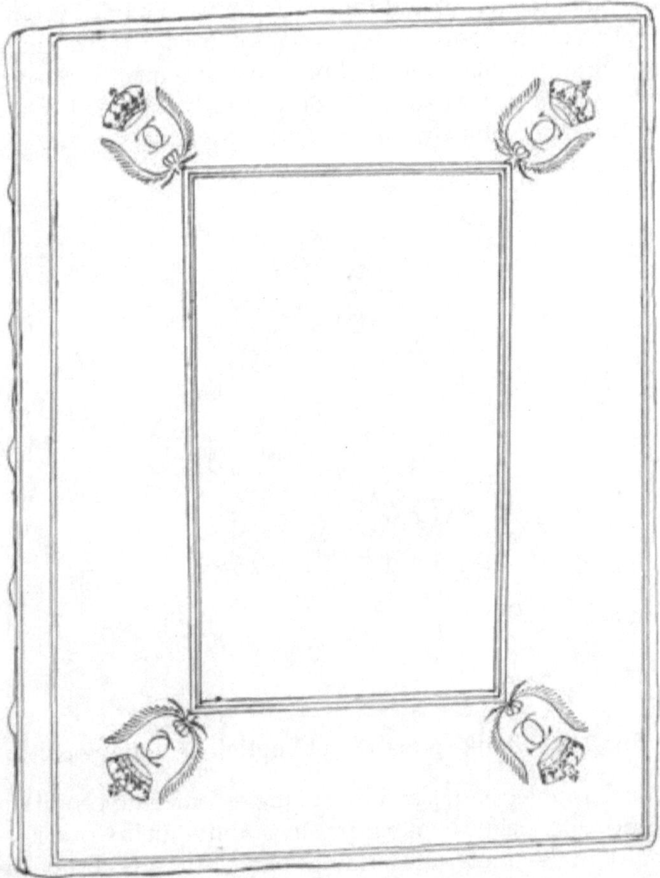

Fig. 115.—English gold tooled "Rectangular" style binding, by Samuel Mearne. Made for Charles II.

Samuel Mearne was appointed royal binder to Charles II., and he was the second great binder in England. Mearne bound the majority of his books in the same beautiful red leather that I have already mentioned as being used for some late bindings belonging to Charles I., and the same coat-of-arms occurs on some of those bound for Charles II. This red leather was probably dyed with cochineal. Before this no red leather was used to any extent in England. Brown, olive, blue, and black were all common, but not red. The ordinary bindings made by Mearne for Charles II. were simply and tastefully ornamented with rectangular lines having the royal initials at the corners, but others are more elaborate.

Fig. 116.—English gold tooled binding by Samuel Mearne.
Made for Charles II.

We owe a national design to Mearne's inventive genius, and it is known as the "Cottage" style. The gold-lined parallelogram is the starting point, and the upper and lower lines are broken outwards into a gable form. From this starting point Mearne developed his further decoration with supreme success, until indeed he succeeded in producing some of the finest bindings for large books that have ever been made. Not only that, Mearne's style and even the details of his stamps continue until the present time, and the Bible on which King Edward VII. took the coronation oath was bound in the Cottage style. No style has ever lasted so long, not only in England, but in any other country.

Fig. 117.—English gold-tooled binding in "all-over" style, by Samuel Mearne.

There was yet another beautiful style invented by Mearne. It is not so real a design as the Cottage, as it partakes to some extent of the principle of the semis, inasmuch as symmetrical repetition is an integral part of it. There is no doubt that Mearne saw and admired the work of the great French contemporary binder Le Gascon, and from him he borrowed several ideas, among them that of the pointille or dotted stamps, and also that of the interlacing fillets with interstitial spaces filled with small gold tooling.

Fig. 118.—English gold tooled binding showing the influence
of Samuel Mearne.

The radical change that Mearne made with regard to Le Gascon's interlacing fillets was that he made them up by using successive impressions of a two-horned curve instead of a continuous fillet or ribbon. Although at first sight there would seem to be no connection between one of these "all over" bindings by Mearne and one of Le Gascon's exquisite little interlacings, I think the connection is undoubted.

The all-over bindings, always small, are not uncommon; they are in black or red morocco, with colours interchanged, and are tooled in gold, with the very decorative addition of silver paint, water-colour, applied by hand here and there.

Eliot and Chapman did much excellent work in the eighteenth century and invented large ornamental borders for their bindings. These borders are not rolls, but the component parts are separately stamped. There is an excellent design with arches, a bird and a fly, and another with a globe, but all of them are admirably and effectively designed.

Except the work of Eliot and Chapman, the main English ornamentations on bookbindings during the eighteenth century were modifications of one or other of Mearne's designs.

Eliot and Chapman bound largely for Robert Harley, first Earl of Oxford, and their broad bordered style is known as the "Harleian." The centres, in the finest examples, are left unornamented, but there are numbers of examples, especially in later work, in which the centres are filled with a diamond-shaped mass of small gold toolings. Their style has been very largely copied.

Fig. 119.—The book stamp of Robert Harley.

Towards the end of the eighteenth century English binding received a remarkable stimulus by reason of the advent of Roger Payne, a native of Windsor, who set up in London as a bookbinder about 1770.

Payne's two predecessors, Berthelet and Mearne, had both enjoyed Court positions, but Payne never did; he worked when he chose, and only then, and even if the brilliancy and genius shown of his work had ever been known to George III., it is doubtful whether so unreliable a man as Payne was could ever have been allowed to hold any responsible position.

Fig. 120.—English gold tooled binding, by Roger Payne.

The main charm of Payne's work consists in the spare ornamentation of beautiful leather with exquisitely designed and cut stamps. These stamps are said to have been cut by himself in iron, but most of them were certainly of brass. One of Payne's stamps only is specially cut so as to be capable of being used in combination; it is a little sprig of vine, and he used it not only by itself, but sometimes so as to make an entire vine oval on the side of a book. Payne was also the first great

English binder to pay much attention to the inside of the boards of his bindings. His "Doublures," as they are called, often show more elaborate work than exists outside the books. The masses of small stamps which occur on the borders of the fine doublures and in the corners of Payne's bindings are arranged in parallel lines, but have little constructive arrangement. The brilliancy of Payne's gold tooling has never been exceeded.

In his simpler bindings Payne used a deep soft purple end paper, usually lined with gold round the edge. The leather joint red or green is also often gilded, and shows a stitch or two of the silk thread which Payne always used. The headbands are small and rounded, of green silk, with sometimes a gold thread here and there.

The colours of Payne's moroccos are deep blue, deep red, orange, deep olive, or pale sea-green. If other colours are found on bindings apparently by him, I should begin by suspecting the work is that of Richard Wier. His Russia leathers are always dull brown in colour, and diced. Payne lined his backs too thickly, and his books often open stiffly. This is not of much importance when the binding is morocco, but when Russia leather is used it causes it to break at the joints. Some of the designs in the back panels of Payne's more decorative bindings are quite admirable. His moroccos are smooth or straight-grained, a method of treating the leather that he invented. Payne often added a manuscript note to his bound work and pasted it in the beginning. Several of these notes are of great interest, as they show the immense care and trouble he took to do the best he could in every case. They are also of the greatest value in showing that certain pieces of work are unquestionably from his own hand.

Richard Wier, a Scottish bookbinder, worked with Payne, and closely copied his style. Wier was fonder of blind tooling than Payne was, and they used the same stamps. Many of the bindings credited to Roger Payne are really by Wier, who, as well as Mrs. Wier, was a highly skilled mender of books.

Charles Hering founded his styles upon those of Payne, but soon evolved a manner of his own. He finished some books that Payne had left unfinished in the same style. Originals and copies are now in the Rylands Library at Manchester. Hering's work is, however, only high class trade binding, as is that of his contemporary, C. Kalthœber. Both Hering's and Kalthœber's work is often signed, either in small gilt or blind lettering along the lower edge of one of the boards, or by an affixed ticket.

Kalthœber frankly copied Payne's styles and stamps, but elaborated both so much that he quite lost sight of the characteristic simplicity of the great master. Kalthœber bound several books for George III., and many of them are decorative enough, and if they had not been such parodies of Payne's work they would no doubt have taken high rank.

Staggemeier and Walther were both Germans, who worked much in the same manner as Kalthœber. They both signed their bindings.

Charles Lewis was very nearly a great binder, but I do not think he quite reached that level. He used flat double bands with gold tooling upon them, but these are frequently only shams, and are in company with hollow backs. After that his best work was borrowed; but his bindings are always pleasant to handle and admirably forwarded and finished. Lewis' headbands are flat and upright, and generally sewn with green silk or red and green silk. He was fond of brilliant doublures, sometimes all gold, sometimes vellum edged with richly gilt morocco, and he was also fond of gilded edges richly tooled.

In the nineteenth century we have in England produced one binder who will probably in due time rank with the highest. The work of Mr. T. J. Cobden-Sanderson will bear comparison with the best work the past can show, either as to general design or beauty of detail. Most of the good art binding done now owes its inspiration to Mr. Cobden-Sanderson, and already many of his pupils and followers have achieved distinction for themselves; one of the best of these is Mr. Douglas Cockerell. The rare work done by Sir Edward Sullivan will also live. He is entirely original in his work and in his manner of decoration.

Lady bookbinders in England have also done excellent and beautiful work, particularly Miss E. M. MacColl, Miss Sarah Prideaux, and Miss N. E. Woolrich.

Professional work of high excellence has been done in recent years in England by Messrs. Bedford, Rivière, Zaehnsdorf, and Morell. The younger Zaehnsdorf, G. Sutcliffe, F. Sangorsky, Fazakerly of Liverpool, and A. De Santy are all reliable, and may be trusted to produce work not only technically perfect, but also charmingly finished and admirably designed.

Compared, however, to modern French professional bookbinding of the first rank, by Capé, Duru, Lortic, Bauzonnet, and the rest, I find that there is a certain heaviness in English forwarding—English binders have always liked heavy boards; but I think that in the matter of gold tooling our best modern finishers can hold their own safely.

Bookbinding has been more fostered and looked after in France than in any other country. As early as 1401 a guild of all persons concerned in book production was founded by charter from Charles VI., and continued, with some changes, until 1791.

The chief change in this guild took place in 1686, when the binding and gilding were treated as separate arts, as, indeed, they properly are. From the time of Francis I. until about 1633 we find that nearly all the Kings of France had official binders, and, as might be expected, the best French work is to be among their work, with the exception of that of Le Gascon, who, like our Roger Payne, was never favoured with Court patronage.

Heraldry plays a considerable part in English bookbinding, but not so remarkable a one as it does in French bookbinding. From royal books downwards, persons of distinction, ecclesiastics of all ranks, ladies and private persons, all liked to have their books ornamented with their coats-of-arms as a principal ornament.

Etienne Roffet was Royal binder to Francis I., but I do not feel sure that any binding of his is known. It may be, however, considered likely that he bound most of the books bearing the King's crowned initials and his device of a salamander.

Several of Jean Grolier's books were bound by French workmen. These are in the main designed on similar lines to those bound by Italians, but there is a difference in the details of the stamps used. One constant difference may be found in the fact that on the Italian books the small leaves and devices are *solid*, and on the French ones they are *azured*, or scored across with fine lines. Some of the French bound books have colour added on the fillets.

Fig. 121.—French coloured and gold tooled binding, with portrait of Henri II.

Geoffrey Tory lived well into the sixteenth century, and among other artistic productions he designed a special stamp for gilding his bindings with. Tory lost his only little daughter, and afterwards adopted as his device a broken vase, symbolic of his broken life. This vase is sometimes pierced by a "toret," probably a play upon his own name, as he describes it: "ung vase antique qui est cassé par lequel passe ung toret." The book stamps do not show the toret, but the vase is there. In the other ornamentation and on these Tory bindings is a strong Italian feeling. It is sure enough that the art of gold tooling reached France by way of Venice, just as it did England.

Fig. 122.—French sixteenth century binding, made for Diane de Poictiers.

The most gorgeous period of French bookbinding was that of Henri II. and his children. Henri himself loved fine bindings, and so did Catherine de Medici, but unfortunately we do not know who executed them. They are in calf or morocco, and nearly always have coloured fillets. Those which were bound for Diane de

Poictiers, Duchesse de Valentinois, are equally remarkable, and all of them have, as a rule, heraldic ornamentation. A fine portrait cameo stamp, however, of Henri II. appears as a centrepiece on some of his bindings, and the name Dianne appears on one of Diane's now in the Bibliothèque Nationale at Paris.

Fig. 123.—French binding by Nicholas Eve, 1578. Made for Henri III.

The cyphers which appear on all these bindings are as a rule straightforward enough, being either those of Henri or his Queen Catherine, but among them is one which contains the initials H. and D. intertwined. This may mean "Henri Dauphin," but it is usually interpreted as meaning "Henri" and "Diane." I do not propose here to enter into the vexed question of this curious cypher, as it has already been fully discussed elsewhere,[1] but I may say that Henri's own device before he succeeded to the throne was a crescent with the legend Nec impleat totem orbem. An unstrung bow as well as the other emblems of Diana the huntress undoubtedly appears on bindings made for this king. I am rather inclined to think that these devices of bow, crescents, and quiver, which show on the bindings made for Henri as well as on those made for Diane de Poictiers, may really have been separately chosen, and have no necessary connection with each other. On the bindings made for Diane de Poictiers the bow is strung.

Henri III. was an eccentric king, and it has been said that among other arts he learnt that of bookbinding. He lost his ladylove, and ever afterwards grieved her loss. His bindings show the device of the confraternity of the White Monks, to which order he belonged, and a skull and "Spes mea deus." But besides these gloomy bindings we owe some of the finest bindings ever made in France to the art of Henri's royal binder, Nicholas Eve.

The French order of St. Michel was founded by Louis XI., in 1466, in place of an older order "De l'Etoile," which had been instituted by Jean II. Henri III., in 1578, founded a new order, the Saint Esprit, and among the State papers of the time is a note to the effect that Nicholas Eve bound forty-two copies of the *Ordonnances de l'ordre du Sainct Esprit* for the king. One of these books is now in the British Museum. It is bound, as described in the official note, in orange morocco, and agrees in all respects with that description.

Fig. 124.—French, gold tooled "Fanfare" binding. Made for J. A. De Thou.

[1] *Anglo-Saxon Review* and *Burlington Magazine*, July, 1907.

A remarkable style, known as "à la Fanfare," became common in France about the end of the sixteenth century. They are generally attributed to Clovis Eve, who was Relieur du Roy (1596), but there is really no authority for such attribution. The style is a beautiful one, and consists of interlaced fillets enclosing graceful sprays of laurel or palm, and arabesque curves. Some of the finest examples were bound for J. A. de Thou, the historian, and bear his arms, a chevron between three gad-flies, as a centre ornament.

Most of De Thou's books are bound in morocco, and among those which were made during the life of his second wife Gasparde de la Chastre are some that are curiously ornamented. They are bound in pale yellow morocco which has been stamped all over with impressions in black outline, probably from a wood block, in floral or conventional designs. The designs have afterwards been filled in by hand with colour stains, green, red and blue. The leather has been cut for the binding without any notice being taken of the coloured designs, which consequently appear irregularly on the finished work. The books are finished with gold lines and the arms of De Thou and La Chastre side by side.

It has been said that De Thou chose certain colours for certain subjects, for the bindings of his books, but although it may be so in some cases I do not think it is consistently carried out.

Certain colours have no doubt been chosen in some cases as distinctive of ownership, as for instance in the libraries of the three daughters of Louis XV., all of whom bore the same coat-of-arms. The books belonging to Madame Victoire were bound in olive, those of Madame Adelaide in red, and those of Madame Sophie in citron.

French bindings in morocco were sometimes stained with colour, especially about the time of Henri II., but colour on morocco is more generally added as a pigment.

In recent times some very decorative Spanish moroccos have been curiously stained with a sort of marbling. Large consignments of these coloured moroccos have been imported into this country, and they have been used especially by Mr. Roger De Coverly, one of our foremost bookbinders. The morocco is not of a very good quality, and it is too early to say whether the stains are harmful to the leather, as they probably would be if they were on calf.

Colour as indicating subject is usually given in the case of large libraries that do their own binding. Red commonly indicates history and art; blue, theology; green, agriculture and botany; and so on.

In the early seventeenth century the mysterious "Le Gascon" invented the "pointillé" or dotted style of gold tooling, which has been more universally copied than any other small peculiarity in book finishing.

Le Gascon was supreme in the binding of small books, whether ornamented with interlaced fillets, inlaid, or with the curious design of a swollen cross. Le Gascon's small pointillé curves are most cleverly designed; two or three of them suffice to cover a considerable space with an apparently complicated design. The glittering effect of the small pointillé work massed together is heightened by the free addition of small golden dots wherever space can be found for them.

French Seventeenth Century binding by Le Gascon. Red Morocco, Inlaid with Olive and Citron Morocco and Gold Tooled in the Pointillé manner.

Red morocco was Le Gascon's favourite groundwork, and on this he frequently set inlays of coloured morocco, citron, olive and marbled brown. These were mostly used in the case of bindings bearing a design of interlacing fillets, with gold tooling between them. No signed binding by Le Gascon is as yet known, but there are some bearing the name of Florimond Badier, who was son-in-law to Jean

Gillède, which nearly resemble Le Gascon's work, but lack his exquisite finish. On some of these appears a small dotted profile head, which is supposed to be a mark of Le Gascon's. This same head is copied on some of the bindings of our English Samuel Mearne, who must therefore have seen and admired some of Le Gascon's or Badier's work. "Le Gascon" was probably Jean Gillède.

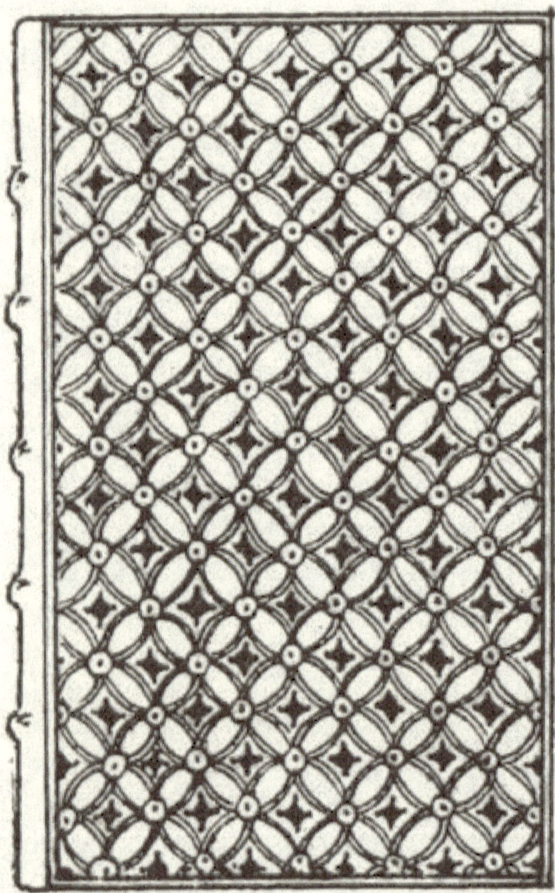

Fig. 125.—French inlaid and gold tooled binding, 1718, by Padeloup le Jeune.

Macè Ruette followed many of Le Gascon's manners, and his son Antoine did the same. These binders were royal binders to Louis XIII. and Louis XIV. respectively, and probably bound most of the fine bindings made for these kings, bearing their coats-of-arms.

The bindings made for the Baron de Longepierre are not uncommon. They were probably bound by Luc Antoine Boyet, royal binder to Louis XV. These little books bear upon them the device of a golden fleece, because the Baron wrote plays, and the only successful one was called "Medea" and dealt with the subject of the Argonauts. The bindings are all exquisitely finished, and of beautiful red leather; they sometimes have finely decorated doublures and marbling under the gold on the edges, a charming detail which has been much liked by French binders ever since.

Padeloup le Jeune was royal binder to Louis XV. after Boyet, and belonged to one of the many French families of binders. Padeloup's work is luckily often signed by means of a small ticket on the title page or end paper. He perfected the patterns known as "Dentelles," which had been first thought of by Boyet. These designs start from the edges of the boards inwards, and the inner edge is deeply dentated and is supposed to resemble lace. Padeloup used blue and red morocco, and executed several small bindings with inlays of coloured leather in geometrical designs.

Fig. 126.—French gold tooled binding "Dentelle à l'oiseau," by Derôme le Jeune.

Padeloup made several large bindings, and his stamps are often large and boldly cut, but his successors gradually fined his style down until the original bold indented work became quite small and lace-like in itself.

The liking for inlaid work which was started by Padeloup rapidly grew, and it caused a certain deterioration in the taste of French binding because it gave such scope for minute technical skill that this soon became more sought after than the power of fine designing. The skill shown on inlaid bindings by Jean le Monnier, for instance, is astonishing, but the designs on all his bindings are weak. The same may be said of the work of J. A. Derôme. But the work of both these binders is much sought after and esteemed by many collectors.

Derôme le Jeune was the most important French binder of the late eighteenth century. He took Padeloup's large "dentelles" and altered them so much that he at last evolved a style of his own from them. Derôme drew the whole design out in a much smaller and more delicate way, and always put in some bird figures, and these designs are known as "Dentelles a l'oiseau." He used citron, olive and red morocco. Derôme has not a good reputation as a forwarder; he is said to have cropped his books badly, and also to have "sawn in" his bands so as to get flat or open backs. Even so, he did not invent "sawn in" bands, as that vice was practised in England a hundred years before Derôme's time, in the case of embroidered books; but the fact of these two mannerisms having been noticed in the work of this great binder only shows that the same faults were probably universally prevalent at the time.

Modern French work is astonishing for its technical skill. The work of Capé, Duru, Thouvenin, Bauzonnet, Trautz, Lortic, Niedrée, Marius-Michel, Chambolle, and many others is admirable from all workmanlike points of view.

But there is no genius in any of it; a great French binder of this century is yet to come.

Spanish bindings are often very handsomely gold tooled, and are usually ornamented with heraldic designs. Little is known at present about them, but it is certainly doubtful whether any great school of gold tooling in bindings has ever existed outside Italy, England or France.

BOOKS TO CONSULT.

ANGLO-SAXON REVIEW.—*London*, 1899. (Articles at the beginning of each vol., by Cyril Davenport.)

BAUCHART.—*See* Quentin-Bauchart.

BERALDI, H.—La Reliure du XIXe. Siècle. *London*, 1895-97.

BERNARD, A. J.—G. Tory. *Paris*, 1857.

BICKELL, L.—Bucheinbände des XV. bis XVIII. Jahrhunderts aus hessischen Bibliotheken. *Leipzig*, 1892.

BOSQUET, E.—La Reliure. *Paris*, 1894.

BOUCHOT, H.—De la Reliure. *Paris*, 1891.

BOUCHOT, H.—Le Livre. *Paris*, 1886.

BOUCHOT, H.—Les reliures d'Art à la Bibliothèque Nationale. *Paris*, 1888.

BRASSINGTON, W. S.—Historic bindings in the Bodleian Library. *London*, 1891.

BRUNET, C. G.—Etudes sur la reliure des Livres. *Bordeaux*, 1891.

BURLINGTON FINE ARTS CLUB.—Illustrated Catalogue of Bookbindings. *London*, 1891.

CUNDALL, J.—Bookbindings Ancient and Modern. *London*, 1891.

DAVENPORT, CYRIL.—Cantor Lectures on Decorative Bookbindings. *London*, 1898.

DAVENPORT, CYRIL.—Bagford's Notes on Bookbinding. *London*, 1894.

DAVENPORT, CYRIL.—Life of Samuel Mearne. *Chicago*, 1907.

DAVENPORT, CYRIL.—Life of Thos. Berthelet. *Chicago*, 1901.

DAVENPORT, CYRIL.—Royal English Bookbindings. *London*, 1896.

DERÔME, L.—La Reliure de Luxe. *Paris*, 1888.

FLETCHER, W. Y.—Bookbindings in France. *London*, 1894.

FLETCHER, W. Y.—English Bookbindings in the British Museum. *London*, 1895.

FLETCHER, W. Y.—Foreign Bookbindings in the British Museum. *London*, 1896.

FOURNIER, E.—L'Art de la Reliure en France. *Paris*, 1888.

GRUEL, L.—Conférence sur la Reliure et la Dorure des Livres. *Paris*, 1896.

GRUEL, L.—Manuel de l'Amateur de Reliures. *Paris*, 1887.

GUIGARD.—Armorial du Bibliophile. *Paris*, 1890.

HOE, R.—One hundred and seventy-two historic bookbindings from the Library of Robert Hoe. *New York*, 1895.

HOLMES, R. R.—Specimens of Bookbindings from the Royal Library, Windsor Castle. *London*, 1893.

HORNE, H. P.—The Bindings of Books. *London*, 1894.

MATTHEWS, J. B.—Bookbindings Old and New. *London*, 1896.

MICHEL, M.—La Reliure Française. *Paris*, 1881.

PRIDEAUX, S. T.—Bookbinders and their Craft. *London*, 1903.

PRIDEAUX, S. T.—Historical Sketch of Bookbinding. *London*, 1893.

QUENTIN-BAUCHART, E.—Les Femmes Bibliophiles de France, XVIe, XVIIe. et XVIIIe. Siècles. *Paris*, 1886.

THOINAN, E.—Les Relieurs Français. *Paris*, 1893.

UZANNE, O.—L'Art dans la Decoration Extérieure des Livres en France. *Paris*, 1898.

UZANNE, O.—La Reliure Moderne. *Paris*, 1887.

WHEATLEY, H. B.—Remarkable Bindings in the British Museum. *London*, 1889.

INDEX

D

Q

R

S

X

Z

Lector House believes that a society develops through a two-fold approach of continuous learning and adaptation, which is derived from the study of classic literary works spread across the historic timeline of literature records. Therefore, we aim at reviving, repairing and redeveloping all those inaccessible or damaged but historically as well as culturally important literature across subjects so that the future generations may have an opportunity to study and learn from past works to embark upon a journey of creating a better future.

This book is a result of an effort made by Lector House towards making a contribution to the preservation and repair of original ancient works which might hold historical significance to the approach of continuous learning across subjects.

HAPPY READING & LEARNING!

LECTOR HOUSE LLP
E-MAIL: lectorpublishing@gmail.com